DEFY
Defian

151 Insights, Strategies, Lessons and Activities for Helping Students
with ODD *(Oppositional Defiant Disorder)*

GRADES K-12

By Tip Frank, Ed.S.   Mike Paget, M.Ed.   Jerry Wilde, Ph.D.

youth light
inc.

© 2012, 2007, 2005 by YouthLight, Inc.
Chapin, SC 29036

Design and Layout by Diane Florence • Project Editing by Susan Bowman

ISBN
978-1-889636-77-1

Library of Congress Number
2004117914

10 9 8 7 6 5 4 3
Printed in the United States

Table of Contents

Acknowledgements

The authors have had the opportunity to work for a number of years with Dr. Robert Bowman. Bob has been a constant inspiration in his deep respect for others and in his never-ending energy for finding positive responses to the challenging behaviors presented by children and youth.

Much of the work on this book happened after lunch at the Front Porch Restaurant in Richburg, South Carolina. Mike and Tip are thankful for the kindness and support given to us by the employees of the Front Porch as they allowed us to work in the back room, continually checking on us to see if we needed more iced tea. We are particularly thankful to the owner of the Front Porch, Libby Gaston, for that wonderful apple cobbler with vanilla bean ice cream!

Preface

The authors of this book all have years of experience working with children and youth who present severe oppositional and defiant behaviors. We have worked as teachers, guidance counselors, clinical psychologists, therapists, and clinical administrators. We share common attitudes about challenging children, and we have learned a great deal from each other in the exploration of the ideas presented in this book.

A consistent theme in the work of all three authors is the desire to find practical solutions to difficult behaviors. It is clear that the adults who work with these children, the parents of these children, and the children themselves are often in great distress. It is also clear that there are things that can be done to improve the situation for all. So, it is the goal of Jerry, Mike, and Tip to share ideas that will make a difference in the lives of these children, and in the lives of those adults who care for them.

Chapter 1

Defining the Defiance

In this chapter we will define the disorder. We will review both formal and informal definitions and descriptions of key characteristics. It is the assumption that insights regarding the definition will help the reader understand the importance and origin of many of the strategies.

Who is the Oppositional Defiant Disorder student, and how did he or she get this way?

"Oppositional Defiant Disorder" (ODD) is a diagnostic label provided by the Diagnostic and Statistical Manual of Mental Disorders (DSM), 4th Edition, American Psychiatric Association. The DSM may be thought of as the "dictionary," or guidebook, for identifying and labeling clusters of emotions and behaviors. It reflects the ongoing efforts of the medical and treatment communities to understand and respond to patterns of behavior that are problematic both for the individual being labeled and for those who are in the "sphere of impact" of that individual.

A DSM classification system is convenient and provides a means of getting a handle on these patterns, at least in terms of predictability. As individuals who have worked with children and youth having the ODD label, the authors take this designation as a starting point, not an end point. It is important to the authors to approach each young person as having the potential to move beyond behavior patterns that cause difficulty both for the youngster and those in that child's life space.

A Little ODD Quiz

Let's put the formal definition aside for a few moments and complete a short questionnaire. Better yet, get with someone you know well and answer the questionnaire together. The questions call for "yes/no" answers. So, let's see how you do!

Have you ever…

❏ Yelled and screamed at anyone?

❏ Been so mad that you fantasized about doing major bodily harm to someone?

❏ Refused to give in when arguing with your teacher or boss, maybe just for the sake of winning the argument?

❏ Responded with an "in your face" attitude to a request by someone to follow a rule?

❏ Found someone's "hot button" and deliberately pushed it?

❏ When no one was looking, damaged someone's property to get back at him or her for something?

❏ Said some bad things about someone to get back at them?

❏ Blamed someone else for a mistake you made?

❏ Had a "chip on your shoulder" or been in a "touchy" mood?

❏ Found yourself feeling angry for days on end about something that may have happened awhile back?

Scoring Your Quiz

If you are like most people, you probably said "yes" to at least a few of these questions. In fact, you may have said yes to a majority of the questions.

You may be interested to know that the questions deal with the eight diagnostic criteria for ODD. Let's look at those criteria. ODD is a pattern of negativistic, hostile, and defiant behavior, including:

1. Often losing your temper
2. Often arguing with adults/authority figures
3. Actively defying or refusing to comply with directives
4. Deliberately annoying others
5. Blaming others for one's mistakes
6. Being "touchy" or easily annoyed by others
7. Often feeling angry or resentful
8. Often being spiteful or vindictive

INSIGHT #1

Frequency, Intensity, and Duration

So, does this mean that you may meet the diagnostic criteria for ODD? Maybe, but not necessarily. However, it may be helpful to realize that the behaviors and attitudes that comprise ODD are common to most people. What distinguishes the average person from someone who could be diagnosed as ODD is frequency, intensity, and duration of these issues.

Formal Diagnosis
To meet the criteria for ODD, one must display at least four of the eight characteristics in a recurrent behavior pattern that has lasted at least six months. For the individual who meets the criteria, there will be a significant impact on social, academic, and employment functioning.

Disruptive Behavior Disorders: ODD's Close Cousins

Oppositional Defiant Disorder has two close cousins. They are Attention Deficit/ Hyperactivity Disorder (AD/HD) and Conduct Disorder (CD). Note the succinct definitions of these three "cousins" below which we call "Disruptive Behavior Disorders."

AD/HD
Attention Deficit Hyperactivity Disorder: "...developmentally inappropriate degrees of inattention, impulsiveness, and hyperactivity"

CD
Conduct Disorder: "...a persistent pattern of conduct in which the basic rights of others and major age-appropriate societal norms or rules are violated"

ODD
Oppositional Defiant Disorder: "...a pattern of negativistic, hostile, and defiant behavior without the more serious violations of the basic rights of others that are seen in conduct disorder"

While these three disorders are different in many ways, there is a lot of overlap as one can see on the following chart. Keep in mind, a child or teen with ODD may also meet the criteria for other disorders. Thus, a clinician may make a dual diagnosis. It is important to look at all the characteristics involved so that proper treatment can be made.

Comparison of Characteristics

	AD/HD	CD	ODD
Inattention:			
Makes careless mistakes	✗		★
Difficulty sustaining attention	✗		★
Does not seem to listen	✗		★
Does not follow through, fails to finish	✗		★
Has difficulty organizing tasks	✗		★
Avoids sustained mental effort tasks	✗		
Often loses things	✗		
Easily distracted by external stimuli	✗		
Often forgetful in daily activities	✗		★
Hyperactivity:			
Often fidgets or squirms	✗		★
Often leaves seat in classroom	✗	★	★
Runs about, climbs excessively, restless	✗		
Difficulty playing quietly	✗		★
"On the go," "driven by a motor"	✗		
Often talks excessively	✗		
Impulsivity:			
Blurts out answers before question	✗		
Has difficulty waiting turn	✗	★	
Interrupts or intrudes on others	✗	★	★
Aggression to people or animals:			
Bullies, threatens, intimidates		✗	★
Initiates physical fights		✗	
Has used a weapon that could harm		✗	
Has been physically cruel to people		✗	
Has been physically cruel to animals		✗	
Has stolen while confronting a victim		✗	
Has forced someone into sexual activity		✗	
Destruction of property:			
Has deliberately set fires to cause harm		✗	
Has deliberately destroyed property		✗	★
Deceitfulness or theft			
Has broken into someone's house, car		✗	
Lies or cons to obtain goods, avoid obligations		✗	★
Has stolen without confronting victim		✗	
Serious violations of rules			
Often stays out late without parental permission		✗	★
Has run away at least twice		✗	★
A pattern of negativistic, hostile, and defiant behavior:			
Often loses temper	★	★	✗
Often argues with adults	★	★	✗
Actively defies, refuses to comply	★	★	✗
Deliberately annoys others	★	★	✗
Blames others for his/her mistakes	★	★	✗
"Touchy," easily annoyed by others		★	✗
Often angry and resentful	★	★	✗
Often spiteful or vindictive		★	✗

Differential Diagnosis

Establishing a differential diagnosis between ODD and other commonly occurring behavioral problems in youth can be a challenging task. This difficulty can be partially attributed to the fact that the diagnostic criteria for ODD have been modified over the years. ODD was first introduced in 1980 in the third edition of the Diagnostic and Statistical Manual of Mental Disorders (DSM-III; APA, 1980; Angold & Costello, 1996). In 1980, the diagnosis of ODD required two out of five behaviors in DSM-III. In 1987 the diagnosis shifted to four out of eight behaviors in the Diagnostic and Statistical Manual of Mental Disorders, third edition, revised (DSM-III-R; APA, 1987). The current requirement is for four out of eight behaviors in the DSM-IV (Angold & Costello, 1996). Some have noted that the deletion of swearing and using abusive language was the major change from DSM-III-R to DSM-IV (Atkins et al, 1996). This change from DSM-III-R to DSM-IV has lead Angold and Costello (1996) to conclude that the "DSM-IV criteria have led to the inclusion of a more disturbed group of children at the expense of dropping a somewhat less disturbed group of children" (p. 1214).

One of the challenges to arriving at a differential diagnosis has to do with the fact that some of the behavioral indicators of ODD are shared with other disorders, most notably CD and ADHD. Some of the key features of oppositional defiant disorder that overlap with conduct disorder include argumentativeness, defiance, and problems with anger management. However, there are important distinctions. Children with oppositional defiant disorder, although argumentative, do not normally display significant physical aggression and by definition do not have a history of violating the basic rights of others. Parents of children with oppositional defiant disorder are more likely to have mood disorders than the antisocial pattern common among parents of children who have conduct disorder. Complicating the matter is the fact that some children and adolescents diagnosed with oppositional defiant disorder eventually are also diagnosed with a conduct disorder. Atkins et al. (1996) noted that research suggests that most children with CD have early histories of ODD, and that there are similar familial patterns for CD and ODD. Similarly, a history of CD is commonly found in adults diagnosed with antisocial personality disorder.

The role that socioeconomic status (SES) plays in the diagnosis of ODD and CD is unclear. However, in a study by Green et al. (2002) it was reported that children diagnosed as ODD had significantly lower SES than psychiatric comparison subjects and that the SES of children diagnosed with both ODD and CD was significantly lower than that of those subjects diagnosed with ODD alone.

As mentioned earlier, children being considered for the diagnosis of ODD can also manifest problems commonly associated with attention deficit hyperactivity disorder (ADHD). Approximately two out of three children diagnosed with ADHD are also suffering from an additional DSM-IV disorder. These are referred to as comorbid indicators. Most common of these comorbid indicators are ODD and CD. In fact, 30-40% of children diagnosed with ADHD will also have ODD (Kuhne, et al., 1997). The difficulty associated with distinguishing between ODD and ADHD is best described using an example. One of the diagnostic criteria commonly associated with ODD is "deliberately annoys people." Children with ADHD often have difficulties waiting their turn and, as a result, can be annoying. How does one tell if annoying behavior is deliberate (as with ODD) or simply the result of ADHD? In other words, is the child driving the behavior (ODD) or is the behavior driving the child (ADHD)? To make this judgment will require time to get to know the child and exceptional clinical skills on the part of the professional.

Some of the newer diagnostic tools may be of assistance when trying to make the determination between ADHD and ODD. Software such as the Connor's Continuous Performance Test (CPT) requires subjects to press a computer key upon the presentation of an individual letter. The lone exception to this requirement is when the letter "x" is flashed on the screen. Subjects are told to refrain from responding to the letter "x" which serves as a measure of their ability to manage impulsivity. The CPT has normative data for both students who have been diagnosed with ADHD and for non-ADHD children and adolescents. The advantage of the CPT is that it is not a scale that is reliant on the impressions of teachers or parents. The performance on the CPT is influenced by the student's ability to focus his or her attention.

The common acting out behavior associated with ODD frequently occurs among children and adolescents with major depression and dysthymic disorder. Approximately 15-20% of children with ODD will have problems with their mood and even more experience anxiety (Kuhne, et al., 1997). Patients with early onset bipolar disorder may exhibit impulsive violations of rules and aggression. Once again, the impulsive behavior could be the result of ADHD, early onset of bipolar disorder, or a desire to deliberately "push buttons." Keep in mind that mood disorders typically include disturbances of sleep and appetite and pronounced affective symptoms, as well as significant alterations in energy and activity levels. These symptoms are generally not associated with children diagnosed with ODD.

The diagnosis of intermittent explosive disorder (IED) should also be considered. IED can only be correctly diagnosed when the child's behavior does not meet the criteria for conduct disorder. The hallmark feature of intermittent explosive disorder is unprovoked, sudden aggressive outburst. Patients with intermittent explosive disorder deny plans to harm anyone but report that they "snapped" or "popped" and, without realizing it, assaulted another person. In children and adolescents with intermittent explosive disorder these episodes are the only signs of behavior disturbance. Other than unplanned acts of aggression, patients with intermittent explosive disorder do not engage in repeated violations of other rules or in illegal behavior such as theft or running away from home.

As stated at the beginning of this section, establishing a differential diagnosis between ODD and other commonly occurring behavioral problems in youth can be a challenge. It is hoped that the information describing the similarities and differences between ODD and similar disorders will assist the reader in this complicated and essential step in the treatment of children and adolescents.

INSIGHT #4

When is Oppositional Behavior Within Acceptable Limits, and When Does It Call for Action?

We have developed a screening device to help you quantify the level of difficulty that a student may be having. Because any of the eight characteristics are annoying, disruptive, and sometimes threatening, when they occur at all it is easy to lose perspective and to think that the problems are constant. The following chart will help you determine the level of oppositional and defiant behavior that a student is displaying.

Please note that the inventory has not been validated. Rather, it is provided as a tool to help in determining the need for further diagnosis and intervention.

ODD Screening Inventory

For each of the following descriptions, circle the number that best describes the child's behaviors.

Characteristic	Never	Sometimes	Sometimes, within the last six months	Often, within the last six months	Often, for more than six months
Loses his/her temper	0	1	2	3	4
Argues with adults	0	1	2	3	4
Actively defies or refuses to comply with requests or rules	0	1	2	3	4
Appears to deliberately annoy others	0	1	2	3	4
Blames others for his/her own mistakes or misbehavior	0	1	2	3	4
Is often touchy or easily annoyed by others	0	1	2	3	4
Is angry and resentful	0	1	2	3	4
Is spiteful or vindictive	0	1	2	3	4

SCORING:
Add the numbers you have circled.

Total: [ ]

0 – 8
No significant oppositional and defiant characteristics

9 – 16
Mild to moderate oppositional and defiant characteristics

17 – 32
Moderate to significant oppositional and defiant characteristics; further medical diagnosis and possible intervention is recommended

INSIGHT #5

The Inside Story

So how does the ODD student see him/herself? I would expect that if this student were to read the eight characteristics of ODD, the reactions would include a number of denials, justifications, and rationalizations. Beyond the list, it is extremely important to step into the shoes of the ODD person and to try to understand the deep and powerful beliefs and motivations of this person. From thinking about and working with ODD students, there are several noticeable attitudes that usually come with them.

- I am equal to those in authority – no one has the right to tell me what to do.
- Yes, I sometimes do the wrong thing, but it is usually your fault.
- When you punish or reward me, I feel that you are trying to control or manipulate me.
- Because I know how much you want me to change, I will be very stubborn about changing behaviors. In spite of experiencing your intended punishments and/or rewards, if I change, it will be on my time and for me!
- My greatest sense of control comes from how I make others feel.

INSIGHT #6

ODD and Authority

Interestingly, the eight characteristics that comprise a diagnosis of ODD are all behaviors or attitudes that only exist in relation to others, principally in relation to authority figures. This reality underscores the importance of the authority figure's own behaviors and attitudes in determining how instructive or destructive the situation with the ODD student will become. In that light, the observations given above in the "inside story" (particularly the third and fifth items) are critical to understand and use as guiding principles.

What are the Origins of ODD?

If you work with one or more ODD children, you probably are thinking, "I don't care where it comes from...I just want it to go away!" That perspective is certainly understandable! However, a little insight into the origins sometimes helps an individual understand the significance of some recommended interventions.

INSIGHT #7

Temperament

One possible starting point for this pattern of behavior is simple physiology. Children are born with a range of temperaments. Some children are, by nature, slow to respond, and easy to settle. Others are anything but. We have labels for some of the more persistent patterns, including ADHD. It has been noted that many children start with the ADHD label; but as they get older, they seem to move toward ODD. Other labels often become part of the mix.

INSIGHT #8

Behavior Learned While Being Parented

When a child presents a challenging temperament, it is easy to understand the difficulty this causes in parenting. Without intending such an outcome, parents may unintentionally encourage a persistently negative pattern of behavior. Knowing that their child is difficult to deal with, parents may avoid this daunting process until they cannot stand the intensity any longer. When they do step in to take action, the parents may overreact and then walk away in exasperation. Over time, the child learns to "hang tough" and may begin to feel powerful and successful at getting his or her way.

INSIGHT #9

Unresolved Emotional Issues

Part of the human experience is experiencing a range of emotions. The feelings that we first label as "happy, mad, or sad" take on many colors and intensities. With help and support, we learn to absorb the experiences, to integrate them into who we are and how we are. We develop cognitive, emotional, and behavioral skills for handling our experiences and our emotions. However, sometimes we are unable to easily do so. We become embroiled in a complex of emotions, affecting our thoughts and behaviors. Because some things are just so hard to work out, children sometimes begin to act out those complex emotions. And sometimes that acting out begins to form a pattern that gets labeled as ODD.

The value of understanding possible causes for ODD lies in the possibility it opens up for helping the young person to develop more adaptable and successful behaviors and personal skills.

Following is an extended explanation on another likely source of oppositional and defiant behavior patterns, depression.

The Hidden Cause:
Depression in Oppositional Defiant Disorder

It is easy to overlook depression as a causative factor in the misbehavior of oppositional and defiant children. The focus can become fixated on the behavior rather than the cause of the conduct. However, it is essential that practitioners first understand what's driving the actions before attempting to help children manage their behavior. If depression is the primary cause for the misbehavior, it only makes sense to treat the depression rather than focusing on the behaviors in question. Otherwise the primary source of the problem will be left untreated.

A majority of children and adolescents diagnosed with oppositional defiant disorder (ODD) could be described as externalizers, which explains the commonly used term "acting out." However, there are thousands of ODD students who are also suffering from an internalizing disorder, namely depression. A review of studies on this topic found 21% to 83% of ODD children were also suffering from a depressive disorder (Angold & Costello, 1993). While there is considerable variance in the rates of depression cited among the various studies, one thing is clear. Even at the low end of the spectrum (i.e., 21%), there are still thousands of ODD children battling depression and many with little or no support.

Following is a list of characteristics thought to be associated with depression.

- irritability
- feelings of hopelessness and worthlessness
- references to suicide (i.e., "I'd be better off dead", "Nobody would care if I wasn't around"
- loss of energy
- change in sleep patterns, either waking up early and not being able to get back to sleep or wanting to sleep all the time
- significant change in weight
- loss of interest in normal dating behaviors
- giving away prized possessions
- interest in death (i.e. reading books on death)
- decrease in physical activity
- uncontrollable crying
- excessive guilt
- loss of interest in activities that were previously pleasurable

It is important to note that a significant number of ODD children do not present many of the classic symptoms mentioned above. They may not appear to feel sad or worthless which is why they are often misdiagnosed or go completely undiagnosed. They often come across as simply noncompliant.

Depression and Anger

The most common behavioral manifestation of depression in some children is anger. These clients cover their feelings of worthlessness with rage and often aggressively act out their anger. They can often be found at school in the principal's office because they are constantly in some sort of trouble due to fights or difficulties getting along with teachers and peers.

There is still another substrate of depressed clients who may not even exhibit the above mentioned unmodulated hostility. It's not that these children aren't angry, it's just that they aren't as comfortable expressing their anger and frustration. They exhibit other behaviors that are negative predictors of adjustment such as:

1) cruelty to animals
2) pyromania
3) encopresis

This small cluster of behaviors is also indicative of other serious disorders, but be aware that many of these clients are also depressed.

 INSIGHT #12

A Deeper Understanding of Depression

The brilliant cognitive therapist Aaron Beck postulated three primary beliefs that lead to depression. Beck and Shaw (1977) referred to these beliefs as the "cognitive triad."

1. Negative View of the Self

Typical self-talk from depressed clients who share this personal philosophy includes the following:

"I am no damn good, and I never will amount to anything."
"I deserve the rotten treatment I get."
"No matter what I do, I will fail."
"I can't do anything right."
"Nobody could love me because I am worthless."

There is another interesting phenomenon associated with children who suffer from these types of beliefs. They have a tendency to blame themselves excessively and take responsibility for failures that were not necessarily their fault. The team they play on loses and these children think, "It's probably my fault we lost because I was on the team. If I had only hit a home run every time I had gone up to bat, we might have won."

What is more interesting is when these children do succeed, they often feel they deserve none of the credit. Depressed clients often will not accept recognition for their hard work and prefer to explain the outcome as merely "luck." This type of thinking is emotional double jeopardy. If they fail a test they believe, "This proves how dumb I am." If they receive a high score they think, "Boy, was I ever lucky."

2. Negative View of the World

Not only do depressed children feel they are hopeless, many feel the world is hopeless as well. They seem to think the problems in the world are beyond repair.

"What's the point of going on?"
"You have to watch your back because people are out to take advantage of you."
"Any day now, the world is going to end. It can't go on like this."

3. Negative View of the Future

Many depressed children believe the unfortunate circumstances they are currently experiencing will continue forever. Many look into the future and see nothing but darkness and more difficulties.

"There is no way out."
"I'll never get over this."
"I can't change the horrible things that have happened to me in the past so I'm doomed forever."
"Life sucks now and will always suck."

It is important to realize that there are many corollaries from the three core irrational beliefs contained in Beck's cognitive triad. Numerous variations exist but all seem to have originated from one of these three. The sample messages printed above are just a few of the irrational beliefs that cluster around these core cognitions leading to depression.

Finding Depression in ODD Children

So what can mental health experts and educators do to make certain they don't "miss" depression as a causative factor in oppositional behavior? The first step has already been accomplished by the readers. It's important to **know** there is a high rate of depression (between 21% and 83%) associated with ODD.

Secondly, when working with oppositional youth, **assume** there is depression until you can rule it out. Use Beck's cognitive triad of depressive thinking and simply ask the child or adolescent if he or she believes any of the statements to be true. (Example: "Do you ever think you're worthless or unlovable?" and "Do you ever believe the world is a totally rotten place, and it's never going to get any better?") While it is true some of these kids can be very closed off and even dishonest about their feelings, there are a lot who are just waiting for the questions to be asked. They would be very willing to open up, but no one has bothered to try.

Finally, there are depression inventories that only take a few minutes to complete that can be used as a type of "depression screening." The Beck Depression Inventory (BDI) is used with respondents fourteen and older, and The Children's Depression Inventory (CDI) can be used for younger students. Even though these instruments are relatively short and only take a few minutes, they are still reliable indicators of depression.

When dealing with depression, it is important to help clients analyze the thoughts that sabotage their lives because the beliefs they hold about themselves have as much, if not more, to do with their day-to-day functioning than any other variable. The real secret is not in getting children and adolescents to merely **feel** better because that will allow only limited relief. After the depression is recognized, the challenge lies in helping kids think better.

Overview of the Book

Now that we have a bit of a road map that describes what ODD is and what some of the causal factors may be, we will begin to identify interventions. This book is organized into five chapters. In the first chapter we have just described the condition.

The second chapter focuses on preventative interventions. Preventative interventions may be thought of as foundation interventions. The interventions are useful in work with all oppositional students, are more preventive in nature, and by themselves are usually not enough.

Chapter three moves to moderate interventions. These tools may be viewed as more proactive attempts to avoid periods of escalation. Chapter four describes the more focused and persistent techniques. Finally, chapter five focuses on the most intense attempts to assist the ODD student.

Please note that any and all of the interventions may be needed concurrently. As the parent or teacher, you do not need to work through the interventions in order! You will need to layer and repeat many of the interventions as you provide the structure and circumstances for the young person to develop personal skills. As you begin to sense the pulse of the ODD student, you will find numerous opportunities to expand beyond the 151 numbered techniques in this book!

Chapter 2

First Step: Preventative Interventions

Imagine living in a lovely house in a beautiful valley. The only problem is that you are constantly having to soak up the water that continues to seep under your front door. The reasonable thought to have is, "Why is water flowing under my front door?" And the reasonable improvement in conditions is to go upstream and address the problem at its source!

Supporting good behavior for all students is a bit like this metaphor. In too many schools, our focus is on soaking up the water instead of dealing with the source of the water. This chapter deals with mild interventions. Mild interventions set the climate for success and deal with problems before they happen.

For ODD students the major challenge to the notion of prevention lies in the skill these students have at getting adults off track. A common source of power for the oppositional student is the control he or she has over others' emotions. They are good at pulling our emotional strings. As we become more emotional, we become less rational about our decision-making. For that reason, a part of this chapter addresses the issue of adult attitude and emotional control.

Multimodal Treatment

A well-developed treatment plan is necessary for oppositional-defiant children and teens. This treatment plan involves three distinct areas: assessment, environment setting, and life skills. All three are needed for successful treatment. While ODD is a persistent condition, an early and consistent treatment plan offers the best chance for success.

Assessment

There is always a reason behind the behaviors that people display. When it comes to negativistic, hostile, and defiant behaviors, it behooves us to look for and treat the root causes. So often with ODD-type behaviors, learning and/or medical problems are involved. A child or teen who is unduly struggling with school performance will likely display anger and frustration. Likewise a child or teenager who has a neurological problem or some other physical problem such as depression, bipolar disorder, ADHD, anxiety, vision, hearing, diabetes, etc. will also display angry, noncompliant behaviors. To get at the root causes, careful assessment needs to take place in two ways. The first is a full psychoeducational evaluation; and secondly, a complete medical evaluation is warranted.

Psychoeducational Evaluation

It is a wise idea to have a thorough psychoeducational evaluation done. This can be accomplished most economically through the school system. It can also be done through a private agency. Possible learning disabilities can be detected in this evaluation. Information gained from the psychoeducational evaluation can be used for fine-tuning instruction to meet the student's specific needs. A plan of action on the school's part to meet individual needs is often necessary. In some cases, students qualify for an Individualized Education Plan (IEP) or an Individualized Accommodations Plan (504 Plan) when it is clear that a handicapping condition such as AD/HD or LD (learning disability) is adversely affecting educational performance.

Medical Evaluation

Kids with ODD may have physical problems, chemical imbalances, or a predisposition to mental illness. Douglas Riley in his book *The Defiant Child* writes, "ODD does not cause other disorders or vice versa. However, they often occur hand-in-hand." The following is a list of conditions that can contribute to ODD-type behaviors. This is by no means an exhaustive list.

Biological Conditions
- Adrenal gland abnormalities
- Allergies
- Anemia
- Bacterial infections
- Brain cysts (found rarely in children but possible)
- Brain tumors (found rarely in children but possible)
- Carbon monoxide poisoning
- Cardiac conditions (can reduce the supply of blood, oxygen, and nutrients to the brain)
- Diabetes (early-onset diabetes)
- Drug use (both prescription and illegal can cause certain side effects that mimic AD/HD)
- Fetal alcohol syndrome
- Genetic defects (i.e., fragile X syndrome, sickle cell anemia, Turner's syndrome, etc.)
- Hearing problems
- Heart disease
- Hypoglycemia, improper diet and malnutrition
- Iron deficiency

- Lead poisoning
- Mercury (high level exposure can be related to dental fillings and tooth grinding)
- Metabolic disorders
- Seizure disorders
- Sensory integration dysfunction (over or under sensitivity to touch, taste, smell, sound, and sight)
- Spinal problems (spine and brain not connected properly)
- Thyroid (hyper or hypothyroidism)
- Toxins (i.e., pesticide-poisoning, disinfectants, air fresheners, different types of dusts, etc.)
- Traumatic brain injury (TBI)
- Viral infections
- Vision problems
- Vitamin B deficiencies
- Vitamins (excessive amounts of vitamins can be toxic to the body)
- Worms (pinworms, roundworms, hookworms, and tapeworms)

Psychological Conditions

- Adjustment Disorder
- Anxiety Disorders
- Bipolar Disorder
- Central Auditory Processing Disorder
- Conduct Disorder
- Depression
- Disorder of Written Expression
- Disruptive Behavior Disorder
- Expressive Language Disorder
- Insomnia
- Intermittent Explosive Disorder
- Mathematic Disorder
- Mixed Receptive-Expressive Language Disorder
- Obsessive Compulsive Disorder
- Oppositional Defiant Disorder
- Pervasive Developmental Disorders (autistic spectrum disorders – e.g., Asperger's Syndrome)
- Posttraumatic Stress Disorder
- Reactive Attachment Disorder
- Reading Disorder
- Sleep Disorders
- Tourette's Disorder

Qualified professionals such as psychiatrists, pediatricians, family physicians, psychologists, licensed professional counselors and social workers among others can evaluate if mental or physical problems are in play. All involved with ODD youth should keep in mind to handle them with care. There is a likelihood that more than just bad behavior is involved. A careful physical and mental evaluation is warranted.

Environment Setting

Much of this book is dedicated to how adults in positions of authority can set an environment that is conducive to improving the behaviors of youth with ODD. Environment setting involves developing an effective discipline plan both at home and at school. While there are numerous discipline strategies offered in this book, special care is taken to emphasize the relationship between the adult and child or teenager. One of the basic beliefs of kids with ODD is that adults cannot be trusted. As consistent unconditional regard is established and maintained, behaviors tend to improve over the long haul. Keep in mind, ODD kids will often test adults early and often in a relationship to check out how they will respond. As adults stay on course with consistent boundaries and respectful attitudes, rapport is gradually developed. Dr. Josh McDowell summed this up beautifully by saying, "Discipline without a relationship leads to rebellion" (Promise Keepers Conference, Charlotte, NC, 2001). Solid disciplinary techniques, as presented in this book, along with a real effort to reach out to these youth will often pay off. Essentially, kids with ODD are saying, "You can't control me, but I can be influenced."

Life Skills

Also, at the heart of this book are life skills that need to be instilled in youth with ODD. These life skills are not necessarily developed naturally. They need to be taught and practiced over and over. Kids with ODD often don't develop the skills of handling emotions and relationships well. Through active teaching and counseling, these skills can be imparted to young people. Life skills include impulse control skills, anger management skills, decision-making skills, and social skills.

A developmental guidance approach is emphasized here. This involves giving youth information and skills that they can tap for the rest of their lives. A person who can handle frustration and knows how to get along with others will likely be successful in life.

Basic Building Blocks for Success

The bad news is that Oppositional Defiant Disorder (ODD) is a persistent pattern of negativistic, hostile, and defiant behaviors. The good news lying beneath behaviors is that these are kids that are sensitive, intelligent, and capable. Our challenge as parents and professionals is to unlock the great potential within these strong-willed children and teens. In this light, the title of this book—*Defying the Defiance*—is quite intentional. From the beginning, the message is that nothing is to be gained by defying the child.

As a backdrop on how to unlock this potential and how to redirect these abrasive behaviors, two general building blocks are recommended. These building blocks are mindsets that can and often do evade the negativistic, hostile and defiant behaviors.

Safe Haven
The first building block involves making every effort to provide a safe haven where all kids feel accepted and a part of things. This is a tolerance zone where everyone regardless of his or her background and differences feels included. (This does not mean all behaviors are acceptable, as we will be discussing throughout this book.)

Being a part of a good cause and good group makes all the difference. As one examines tragic events involving school violence such as what took place at Columbine High School, one important common thread among many others is the issue of disenfranchisement. When a student (person) doesn't feel a part of a good cause or purpose, what happens? He or she tends to identify with a deviant peer culture. Hence, antisocial, angry, and aggressive behaviors tend to breed. If a safe haven with positive relationships can be built, the likelihood of bringing out positive behaviors is greatly increased.

Predictable Environment
When children and teens know their boundaries, they feel secure. A predictable environment helps kids to feel safe and settled. A special effort is needed to ensure a sense of fairness and routine. School and home procedures often need to be practiced over and over, but when they are assimilated into the normal way of life, a secure and peaceful feeling occurs. These procedures are more important than ever in our schools when we take into account what is occurring in our culture. Consider the following statistics from The Children's Defense Fund's <u>Leave No Child Behind: Key Facts About American Children, Aug. 2004 data</u>:

- 1 child in 3: is born to unmarried parents
                 is behind a year or more in school
- 1 child in 4: lives with only one parent
- 1 child in 5: is born to a mother who did not graduate from high school
- 1 child in 8: is born to a teenage mother
- 1 child in 24: lives with neither parent

These are just a few statistics that point out just how unsettled it is for so many of our kids. Consistent adults in the lives of kids who offer a sense of stability can often be the tonic many kids with ODD need.

The Need to Develop a PREP

It has been said that on any given day, nearly one in three people are not coping well. This can be a dangerous combination if the adult in charge of a kid or kids with ODD is having a bad day. What is not needed is too much emotion. ODD kids especially pick up on the moods and body language of adults. Adults have to be adept at disengaging and avoiding unnecessary conflict. This, however, is very difficult to do unless an extra effort is taken to take care of ourselves as parents and professionals on a regular basis. To consistently and effectively deal with the ODD child or teen, a "PREP" is recommended.

PREP stands for Personal Reduction of Emotions Plan. A PREP involves two distinct disciplines. If parents and professionals do these two things on a regular basis, the response from ODD kids will likely be more positive. In addition, utilizing a PREP is a good model for how it is hoped kids with ODD will respond under the pressures of life.

The first aspect of a PREP is called maintenance. This involves having two or three outlets for managing stress. Think of yourself as having three distinct tanks that need to be continually filled much in the same way a car needs gas. The three tanks are physical, emotional, and spiritual. If any of these tanks gets near empty, a person is negatively affected. How well do you keep your tanks full? These are three critical areas of life that shouldn't be shortchanged in order to have the energy and poise needed for handling difficult kids. Think of one or more activities for each tank in your life.

Physical

1._____

2._____

Emotional

1._____

2._____

Spiritual

1._____

2._____

The second area of the PREP is immediate stress reduction. When a kid with ODD is acting out, how well do you cope? Dr. Thomas Phelan in his *1-2-3 Magic* book states that the two most common errors made when disciplining youth are too much talk (escalating to yelling) and too much emotion. The goal is to respond—not react. To respond in a dispassionate and rational way, the adult in charge has to have a way to reduce stress when the pressure mounts. This may involve anything from positive self-talk or squeezing a stress ball to prayer, deep breathing, etc. Note the importance of rational self-talk on the following page.

What are some immediate stress relievers for you? Please think of two or more immediate stress relievers and put them to use when the next challenge comes your way.

Immediate Stress Relievers

1._____

2._____

Beliefs Educators Hold

A key component of a personal reduction of emotions plan involves how well the adults in charge can think rationally. When emotions take over, negative consequences typically result. Conversely, rational thinking allows the adult in charge not to get enmeshed in the situation and to handle it well. Note the different ways of thinking below. How clear minded are you?

The beliefs educators hold about their jobs and the students they teach largely influence their feelings, attitudes and behavior. These beliefs can be irrational and self-defeating or rational and life-enhancing. Dr. Gary Alderman, currently a professor of psychology at Winthrop University in Rock Hill, South Carolina, identified a number of common beliefs that educators are susceptible to:

1. *"Unless my students and the staff approve of me, it proves I'm inadequate as an educator,"* rather than the rational belief, *"It would be nice if my students and staff approved of me, but if they don't, I can still do a good job."*

2. *"If I fail as a teacher, I fail in life,"* rather than the rational belief, *"My skills as a teacher and my value as a person are two different things."*

3. *"I have to be respected and I must never be challenged in class,"* rather than the rational belief, *"Having the students' respect is nice but not an absolute necessity. It's uncomfortable to*

   be challenged but it's happened before and I've survived."

4. *"I can't stand it when my class becomes out of control,"* rather than the rational belief, *"It's embarrassing and frustrating when my class gets out of control, but it's not the end of the world."*

5. *"Because things are not going well now, it's probably going to get worse,"* rather than the rational belief, *"Just because things aren't going well now doesn't mean they are going to get worse. It's more likely that they'll get better."*

6. *"Some of these students are bad little kids who deserve to suffer,"* rather than the rational belief, *"There is no such thing as a bad little kid, only kids who ACT badly. Most students misbehave occasionally but that doesn't mean they should suffer."*

As the adult, it is critical that you are able to stay focused and rational when in the presence of a child with ODD. The consequences of falling victim to the irrational thoughts given above include feeding into the unhealthy perspectives of the ODD child, as noted in the first chapter of this book.

Additional Consequences: The Neurochemical Effects of Anger and the Fight or Flight Response

How important is it to handle stress well? Just as it is important to reduce stress for the sake of difficult kids, it is equally important for your health. When one is constantly under stress, he or she is more vulnerable to the common cold, cancer, depression, anxiety, and heart problems, among others. It is a social deterrent as well. No one likes to be around a stressed out person! Dr. Redford Williams in his book *Anger Kills: Seventeen Strategies for Controlling the Hostility That Can Harm Your Health* clearly explained the long-term results of carrying too much stress, anger, or hostility. Please note the anatomy of a heart attack that follows according to Dr. Williams.

Anatomy of a Heart Attack

- A fear or anger provoking experience leads to . . .
- Your body prepares to respond by "fight or flight" . . .
- Your adrenal glands secrete adrenaline and cortisol which causes . . .
- Your heart to pump faster to bring . . .
- "Needed" blood to the muscles around the body for the anticipated flight or fight . . .
- Blood normally destined for the skin, kidneys and intestines is re-routed as the priority is set for muscle action
- Your immune system goes into a holding pattern pending the expected fight/flight
- The resulting high blood pressure may cause an erosion of endothelial cells which line the coronary arteries
- Platelets (clotting elements) hurry to the "damaged" area of the artery (useful if there were a cut from a saber-toothed tiger)
- To provide energy for the "fight," fat cells are released into the blood . . . where the excess ones (most of them) end up being converted by the liver into cholesterol which may collect on the artery walls. . .
- Which may evolve into arteriosclerotic plaque . . .
- Which may one day become a plug that causes a loss of blood to an area of the heart...

HEART ATTACK!

Keeping Yourself Stable

ODD students thrive on your instability. Seeing an authority figure erupt emotionally or physically is extremely reinforcing for the ODD student. For your health, and for your effectiveness, you need ways to stay on a good "emotional TRACK."

Training, planning, being prepared

Rehearsing, practicing, thinking through how you might handle it

Ask for help, support from others—rely on your team

Cues—look for signs that a problem may be developing; it is much easier to head something off at the pass than it is to deal with a full-blown crisis incident. Respond early to the "red flags."

Keep aware of your own instincts and skills—don't overreact

Keep Your Sense of Humor

Some people are naturally more "humor-inclined" than others, but it is possible to improve your HIQ (humor intelligence quotient)! Humor is not sarcasm, and it does not mean making fun of others; but it often means seeing the humor in your own self. To do so requires being comfortable with your faults and mistakes and not taking yourself too seriously. On the caution side, humor does not involve put-downs of others or laughing at someone else's expense.

How can you improve your HIQ? Read humorous articles and stories. Watch funny movies and television shows. Tell funny stories. Coach yourself at seeing irony and paradox in your daily activities. Finally, in extreme humor-deprivation situations, take the approach of playing a role. You may be convinced that you do not have a sense of humor, so give yourself permission to at least act funny for short periods of time. Practice smiling and laughing. And don't be surprised if you discover your own sense of humor.

Avoid Disliking the ODD Student

Sure you say...but this really is important! One strong drive of the ODD student is to fight with you, to oppose. If you readily join in the battle, the focus will usually be on the fight. Rather than finding yourself opposing the student, work at being calm and neutral when they are oppositional.

You may be asking yourself, "How do I like someone who is so unlikable?" With difficult students our experiences cause us to prepare for the next conflict. Based on what has been occurring, we have good reason to expect bad things. So, when we encounter this student, we are mentally prepared for conflict, and we behave in ways that anticipate the conflict. Likewise, the student is probably also anticipating and preparing for more of the same. Some find that, in order to break from this "defiant dance," it helps to consciously create non-conflict experiences with the student. For example, ask the student to join you in some neutral activity, such as walking to the snack area. Engage in new conversation, ask about an interest of the student. If you begin to build non-conflict times, you may find that there are likable characteristics in the student.

INSIGHT #24

Practice Emotional Neutrality

The ODD student watches how you respond to his or her behavior. If you show emotional investment, the ODD student will be reinforced for his or her behavior. The person in charge must be professional while maintaining emotional neutrality. Remember, one of the student's driving motivations is, "My greatest sense of control comes from how I make others feel."

For many, the greater challenge may be refraining from overly enthusiastic responses when the student does something correctly. If the ODD student thinks you may have strong emotional responses of any kind, he/she may be inclined to use your emotion against you by behaving in a way so as to influence you to become emotional.

Avoid Becoming the Most Desirable Target

The ODD student gains a sense of power by affecting the emotions of others. Imagine how much power that is when the "other" is the most authoritarian person around! Be careful not to become that person! You need to have authority without being authoritarian. To do so, focus on staying on track, following through, and avoiding a "Because I said so" attitude.

The Sailor Approach: Untie these NOTS

ODD students are very accustomed to being the MVP – The Most Visable Provoker. Adults may easily gravitate towards giving off numerous rejection notices to the ODD student. Find the focus to make the student feel wanted and valued. Untie these nots!

- Not being overly chastised
- Not being rejected
- Not being labeled as a failure
- Not being judged as hopeless
- Not being treated with indifference

In order to use the sailor approach, you have to chart a conscious path through these oppositional waters. This will not happen without deliberate planning, self-rehearsal, and the desire to continue to be optimistic about this student's possible successes. It takes intentional decisions to behave differently, especially with students who are talented at pushing your "hot buttons."

Plan to Address Each Student's Innate Human Needs in Your Classroom

Many personality theorists have provided explanations about human behavior based on models of personality development that include specific innate needs. One such model is described by authors Larry Brendtro, Martin Brokenleg, and Steve Van Bockern in an article entitled, "The Circle of Courage" (*Beyond Behavior*, Winter, 1991). Based on Native American child rearing values, the authors explain that all (students) need to experience:

Belonging – Regardless of the behavior and attitudes presented by the ODD student, every effort should be made to include the student as an important member of the class.

Competence – The first and most powerful behavior management tool for all students is academic competence. Focus on skill development, regardless of behavior concerns.

Independence – Providing choices and encouraging independent thinking and exploration are natural classroom methods of supporting independence. For ODD students, the use of choices is a natural fit for the inherent desire of this student to have control.

Generosity – All students, including the ODD students, have a need to be needed. Peer tutoring and service learning are two common practices that support generosity. For the ODD student, pay attention to naturally occurring generosity. For example, ODD students are sometimes much more appropriate with younger children. Their charisma and leadership abilities may be seen with a more appreciative audience. You may find that allowing the ODD student the opportunity to be a peer helper or volunteer in a younger class will be a successful and appropriate experience for him or her.

INSIGHT #28

Problems with the Punishment Paradigm

The traditional approach to addressing problem behavior through a punishment approach shows little positive results with complex or troubled students. Some of the punishments that seem to work with generally well-adjusted students include:

- Suspension
- Detention
- Chastisement
- Demerits
- Intimidation through confrontational management

Certainly you could add to this list. For a large number of students these tactics often seem beneficial. The undesirable behavior stops, usually on short order.

However, for challenging students, these techniques are more likely to result in an escalation of inappropriate behavior and a hardening of attitudes on both the student's and the adult's part. *Thankfully, there is solid evidence of other techniques that are highly effective with <u>all</u> students!*

School-Wide Positive Behavior Interventions and Supports

Many of us have experienced the frustration of working with a troubled student in a secluded setting, e.g., a self-contained special education class, or in the guidance office. We successfully teach the student a socially acceptable behavior, then send the student off to use her new skill out in the other areas of the school. Often, it is not too long before the student encounters an adult who relies on the more confrontational approach to management. The results? The student escalates, experiences some restriction or sanction, then is sent back for more help. Over time, the experience is demoralizing for both the student and the helping teacher/guidance counselor.

Positive Behavior Interventions and Supports (PBIS) include a number of clearly defined practices that have been demonstrated to be effective over time. Especially when implemented with a school-wide approach, the practice of PBIS has the potential to significantly improve the behavior of the most challenging student. When all staff members learn PBIS techniques, the student has a much greater chance of being reinforced for appropriate behaviors. While this topic is too detailed for further discussion in this text, the reader is encouraged to explore PBIS. Dr. George Sugai and Dr. Robert Horner, co-directors of the <u>National Technical Assistance Center on Positive Behavior Interventions and Supports</u>, offer a wealth of information on the center's website.

Why is PBIS Especially Important for ODD Students?

The major issues with ODD students are in relationship to authority figures: defiance...resistance...oppositional behaviors. It stands to reason that changing those oppositional dynamics is a key to improving the behavior of ODD students. PBIS is based on adults handling things in significantly different ways, in ways that focus on prevention, instruction, and responding to the right things, instead of always addressing the wrong things. Also, it may be more palatable for the ODD student to receive positive support when it is given in a setting where all students are receiving significant positive feedback. So, because PBIS is good for all students, it is especially beneficial for ODD students.

Positive Behavior Interventions and Supports

Some of the procedures described in the PBIS literature include:
- Functional behavior assessment
- Behavior intervention planning
- 5:1 positive to negative feedback from teachers
- An instructional approach to teaching positive behaviors
- A school-wide agreement on expected socially beneficial expectations
- A school-wide agreement on what those expectations look like in the variety of settings around the school

When these practices become part of the school culture, an increase in positive guidance and a decrease in negative harping become part of the backdrop of the school. For all students, the emotional emphasis moves from negative to positive. For the ODD student, this positive backdrop presents a less obvious target for resistance. Because positive comments and guidance occur all day with all students, the ODD student does not feel singled out in a way that might encourage resistance.

Schools, the Law, and Students with ODD

A primary reason that students are referred to be considered for eligibility as a student with an educational disability is acting out behavior. Separate from any medical diagnosis, students who are persistently resistant, defiant, and generally un-cooperative are likely to be referred. It comes as no surprise, therefore, that ODD children often find themselves identified for special education services. When a student receives special education services, it includes a number of protections and guarantees. Regarding behavior, these guarantees include ensuring that the student is not punished for what may be beyond his or her control. Of course, this gets a bit confusing for the ODD student. One could argue all day with either side of the statement, "Students who are ODD are able/not able to control their behavior." After all, they always look in control, and they do want us to believe that they **are** in control!

Because the characteristics that often cause a student to be referred and identified for special education services are the same characteristics that might later support a medical diagnosis of ODD, it is prudent to assume that special education students with ODD behaviors will remain in school.

Beyond students identified for special education services, students with a medical issue (e.g., ODD) that impacts a major life function (e.g., education) may receive accommodations and legal protections under Section 504 of the Vocational Rehabilitation Act. These "504" students, also, are not likely to be leaving.

Beyond the limitations on suspensions and expulsions, special education law requires that schools use a recognized method of behavior management and change that is named *functional behavioral assessment (FBA) and behavior intervention planning (BIP)*.

Functional Behavioral Assessment

The beginning assumption is that every behavior serves a purpose, or a function. The function may be fleeting, or more deep-seated, but the behavior is doing something for the student. Unless and until that function is figured out, it will be difficult to simply eliminate the undesirable behavior.

There are no quick solutions to oppositional defiant disorder. Patiently looking for patterns and triggers of behavior proves to be fruitful. Note the informal Functional Behavioral Assessment (FBA) that follows. Much rich information can be garnered from this instrument by especially noting the purposes, surrounding circumstances, and consequences of student behaviors. The tendency is to notice only the negative behaviors followed by those interventions that we think will work. This narrow view misses out on much rich information as you can see in the middle of this FBA.

Intervention Codes

Recent special education guidelines regarding addressing discipline and behavior management of children and youth call for the use of a "Functional Behavior Assessment" and "Behavior Plan" approach. The rationale for taking this approach is that specific behaviors serve a purpose for an individual. Discovering the purpose provides the basis for the plan to change the behavior.

The following is a list of intervention codes used in this version of the Functional Behavior Assessment (FBA).

SC: Need to change surrounding circumstances. Changes in school environment, classroom conditions, academic work, peers.

SB: Need for skill building; e.g., social skills, study skills, anger management skills, decision making skills, etc.

BA: Need for behavior analysis and management programs; e.g., (fill in various types of programs including token economy).

PM: Need for peer helping or adult mentoring.
Note: It may be equally helpful to allow the target student to serve as a mentor or tutor.

PI: Need for parental involvement. It may be necessary to involve the parent(s) at the consequence or surrounding circumstance level.

OR: Need for outside referral. Outside agencies and community resources may need to be utilized.

IR: Need for in-school referral. Personnel within a school or district such as counselors, nurses, speech therapists, school psychologists (testing), social workers, behavior specialists, etc. may need to be utilized.

Functional Behavioral Assessment

Specific Behavior(s)		List actions positive or negative

is (are)

↓

Purposeful		What is this person getting out of the behavior?

given

↓

Surrounding Circumstances		When and where do(es) the behavior(s) occur? What seems to trigger the behavior?

which together create

↓

Consequences		What are the results of the behavior?

that need appropriate

↓

Intervention(s) SC PM SB PI BA OR IR		What can be done to encourage improved behavior?

Now follow the FBA and how it might be effective given some typical negative behaviors in the first box. Notice what reasons are behind the student's refusal to follow directions. Thus, the teacher can make some significant changes in his or her approach and avoid triggers that create oppositional behaviors.

Behavior(s)
(negative)

- **Student does not complete task**
- **Student is uncooperative with teacher**
  (argues and refuses to follow directions)

$\downarrow$

Purpose

- **Student is disinterested in task and avoids work**
- **Student wants control**
  (power struggle with teacher)

$\downarrow$

Surrounding
Circumstances

- **Teacher warns student to get to work or he/she will fail the class again this semester**
- **Assignment is a reading and writing activity**
- **Class is just before lunch**

$\downarrow$

Consequences

- **Student is given several verbal reprimands**
- **Student does not complete assignment**
- **Student is removed from class**

$\downarrow$

Intervention(s)

- **SC** Use a variety of learning activities
- **SB** Teach anger management skills
- **BA** Provide reinforcement point system
- **PM** Provide a study buddy
  (peer note taking and time to process new learning)

Not to be overlooked is when the student is complying. What circumstances create an environment that is more motivational? The teacher can look for patterns of success and build on this.

Behavior(s) **(negative)**	• **Student is on task** • **Student relates to peers in an appropriate way**

↓

Purpose	• **Student enjoys activity** • **Student feels successful** • **Student is getting positive attention from peers and teachers**

↓

Surrounding **Circumstances**	• **Activity is hands on** • **Cooperative learning is occurring**

↓

Consequences	• **Student completes assignment** • **Fellow students cooperate with target student**

↓

Intervention(s)	• **Student is successful** • **Reinforce**

Recognize the Likely Functions of Behavior that are Common for ODD Students, and Avoid Unintentionally Reinforcing the Student for Inappropriate Behaviors:

- "I am the equal of those in authority – no one has the right to tell me what to do." De-emphasize "authority" as the reason for a directive (e.g., "the clock says…" instead of "because I said") while emphasizing the choices the student is considering. Acknowledge the student's power to choose.

- "Yes, I sometimes do the wrong thing, but it is usually your fault." Avoid responding to accusations. Focus on the predetermined consequences.

- "When you punish or reward me, I feel that you are trying to control or manipulate me." Emphasize the student's control through choices. Avoid appearing to be invested in the choices.

- "Because I know how much you want me to change, I will be very stubborn about changing behaviors. In spite of experiencing your intended punishments and/or rewards, if I change, it will be on my time and for me." Remain consistent with your consequences (reinforcements and punishments), knowing that it takes time.

- "My greatest sense of control comes from how I make others feel." Train yourself to feel and show an attitude of emotional neutrality when responding to the student.

Frequent Flyer Points

An interesting phenomenon of contemporary life is the opportunity to earn "points" for airline travel, hotel stays, and restaurant visits. The basic idea is that if you pay for the experience enough times, you will eventually get something for "free." So, fly a million miles, and the airlines will let you have a seat (that was statistically anticipated to be empty anyway) for free on a future flight.

Based on the number of such programs, they must be extremely popular, resulting in sufficient increases in business to justify the programs.

For those of you who participate in these programs, do you experience any of the following?

- Collecting the points in and of itself feels satisfying
- Imagining the time at which you will "cash out" motivates you to pile up more points
- And sometimes you realize that you resist "spending" the points, because then you would not reserve the potential to use them in the future

There is a principle at work here. It just may be that the power one has when the points are adding up is rewarding in and of itself. That is, just knowing that you can take that free flight causes you to work hard at getting more spending power, whether or not you actually spend the points.

Realizing that ODD students are highly motivated to have control, this human nature dynamic can be used to develop a "frequent flyer" motivational program for oppositional students. The basic rules are:

- Award points to the students for completion of defined amounts of work.
- Allow the points to be used to "buy out" of a future assignment.
- Let students "bank" the points for that day in the future when they just do not want to work!
- It helps if the students actually receive some tangible item that can be looked at, handled, and valued. Looking at your "stash" is part of the motivational system.

Many schools have successfully used such a system that would allow students to skip homework assignments or certain school assignments. Many of those schools report that students seem to be so motivated by the potential of getting out of something that they rarely "spend" the points.

So, give those ODD students the opportunity to become frequent flyers!

Spacing In (control) vs. Spacing Out (of control)

The physical arrangement of furniture and supplies in a classroom may by utilized as another set of "tools" to help with teaching and managing students.

What you want the space to do	How to use the space
Minimize distractibility	•Consider the impact of lights, sound, visual distractions, heating/cooling
Provide adequate supervision	•Arrange furniture so that you are able to see all students and have them see you
Provide individual support	•Arrange the room so that you have visual, physical, and verbal contact with all students
Provide and teach organization	•Places for storage •Access as needed •Reduction of clutter/distraction •Model individual organization
Provide control of materials	•AV equipment •Materials and supplies for instruction
Personal comfort	•Provide individual territory •Provide distance for students who need relative isolation •Provide social space for relaxed interactions: Dyads, small groups (2 - 3), larger groups •Provide for a variety of kinesthetic/comfort needs: standard desks, tables and chairs, floor sitting, standing
Manage movement	•Do not encourage running •Show safe pathways •Management of exits

Personal Response Style
The effect of your attitude and behaviors

ODD students are tremendously talented at helping the adult forget all he or she ever rationally knew about how to respond to challenging students. For that reason, it is useful to periodically do a self-checkup on your current attitudes and behaviors. The chart below is provided for that purpose. You may want to make copies from the original so that you can revisit this assessment as often as needed.

Checking Up on Myself: Attitudes and Behaviors that Impact

IMPACT ON STUDENTS

	LOW IMPLEMENTATION Escalates Student Behavior		HIGH IMPLEMENTATION Calms Student Behavior		
	1	2	3	4	5
I create a warm tone. Students feel welcomed and encouraged.					
I set clear rules and expectations.					
Consequences are clear and developed in advance.					
I follow through on consequences.					
I handle difficult issues individually and privately.					
I respond angrily and intensely to problems.					
I avoid dealing with problems.					
I remain calm and businesslike when administering consequences.					
I have appropriately high expectations.					
I teach using a variety of strategies and activities.					

Continuous Performance Monitoring

Intermittent reinforcement is the most effective schedule of reinforcement to shape positive behaviors. Staying on task while completing an assignment is a skill that requires much self-discipline and practice. To help students with this skill, a continuous-play signaling tape and pad are used for self-recording. The student self-monitors whether he or she was on task at the sound of each beep on the tape.

For students who resist this method, a similar technique can be used. Say to the student, "Every time the tape beeps, mark down if I (the teacher) am doing something helpful or unhelpful for you." To make this judgment, the ODD student must be paying attention.

This continuous-play signal tape can be easily made or "Listen, Look, and Think" (by Dr. Harvey Parker) can be ordered through ADD Warehouse at (800) 233-9273.

Determining What's Behind the Behavior

A good mental checklist to use includes the four general goals behind misbehavior according to Adlerian psychology. When a child or teen is misbehaving, ask yourself the following.

Power:
- Does this person want more power or control?
- How can I, the adult in charge, allow the child or teen more opportunities to have a sense of control within needed parameters?

Revenge:
- Is this behavior about getting even?
- What is the root of this anger?
- How am I, the adult in charge, being helpful or unhelpful in my approach?

Attention Getting:
- Does the behavior seem to be about getting more of my attention?
- What are some appropriate outlets for gaining more attention?

Inadequate Feelings:
- Is this person "shutting down" because he or she believes the work is too difficult?
- How can his or her self-esteem be increased?
- Do any academic accommodations need to be made?

Risk Factors and Preventative Practices for ODD and Antisocial Behavior
Finding The Building Blocks of Resiliency

Research indicates that most ODD and antisocial behavior develops from a combination of risk factors associated with individuals, families, schools, and communities (Hawkins, 1995; Thornberry, 1994; Gottfredson, 1987). The same factors apply across races, cultures, and classes, and their effects are cumulative. Exposure to multiple and interacting risk factors exponentially increases a child's overall risk (Hawkins, 1995; Thornberry, 1994). Also, antisocial behavior evolves over the course of childhood, often beginning in the preschool and elementary years and peaking in late adolescence/early adulthood. Direct, early intervention can halt its progress; once firmly established, however, antisocial patterns become more difficult to change and can persist into adulthood (Thornberry, 1994; Gottfredson, 1987).

Individual Risk Factors

Several inborn traits and characteristics related to personality, temperament, and cognitive ability have been identified as risk factors for later delinquent behavior. These do not doom children to misbehavior or crime, but they do make them more susceptible to other risks in the environment. In addition, several factors other than inborn traits are known to place individuals at risk.

- Impulsivity
- Inability to adopt a future time perspective or to grasp future consequences of behavior
- Inability to delay gratification
- Inability to self-regulate emotions, especially temper
- The need for stimulation and excitement
- Low harm avoidance
- Low frustration tolerance
- Central nervous system dysfunction
- Low cortical arousal

- A predisposition to aggressive behavior
- Low general aptitude or intelligence
- Exposure to violence and abuse (as either a victim or a witness)
- Alienation
- Rebelliousness
- Association with deviant peers
- Favorable attitudes toward deviant behavior
- Peer rejection
- Early onset of aggressive or problem behavior

(Martinez & Bournival, 1996; Wexler, 1996; Gibbs, 1995; Hawkins, 1995; Wright, 1995; Brier, 1994; Thornberry, 1994; Gottfredson, 1987; Keilitz & Dunivant, 1986).

Family/Community/Societal Risk Factors

Family characteristics, as well as community and societal factors, can increase risk for antisocial behavior.

- Economic deprivation and unemployment that limit access to food, shelter, transportation, and health care
- Parental history of deviant behavior
- Favorable family/community attitudes toward deviant behavior
- Harsh and/or inconsistent discipline
- Poor parental and/or community supervision and monitoring
- Low parental education (especially maternal education)
- Family conflict
- Disruption in care giving
- Out-of-home placement
- Poor attachment between child and family
- Low community attachment and community disorganization, as evidenced by low parent involvement in schools, low voter turnout, and high rates of vandalism and violence
- Parental alcoholism
- Social alienation of the community
- Availability of drugs and guns
- High community turnover
- Exposure to violence, including violence in the home, community, and media
  (Hawkins, 1995; Thornberry, 1994; Gottfredson, 1987)

School–Related Risk Factors

An array of school factors can be linked to delinquent behavior.
- Academic failure beginning in elementary school
- Poor academic aptitude test scores, especially in reading, beginning in Grades 3 and 4
- Lack of commitment to school
- Lack of belief in the validity of rules
- Early aggressive behavior (in Grades K–3)
- Lack of attachment to teachers
- Low aspirations and goals
- Peer rejection and social alienation
- Association with deviant peers, including grouping antisocial children together for instruction and/or punishment
- Low student/teacher morale
- School disorganization
- Ineffective monitoring and management of students and poor adaptation to school, as evidenced by retention and attendance rates, assignment to special education, and student reports of not liking school, lack of effort, alienation, and punishment (Hawkins, 1995; Thornberry, 1994; Gottfredson, 1987; Gottfredson, 1986)

Chronic school failure demoralizes children, can cause loss of status and rejection by peers, destroys self–esteem, and undermines feelings of competence. As a result, it can undermine a child's attachment to teachers, parents, school, and the values they promote. It also generates hopelessness and helplessness. Children cease to believe that their efforts make a difference in outcomes (Brooks, 1994; Brooks, 1994; Brooks, 1992).

In addition, an analysis of disruptive behavior in 600 schools revealed that schools with discipline problems tend to be large and urban; lack teaching resources; lack fair, clearly stated, consistently enforced rules; have students who do not believe in the rules; lack leadership and cooperation among staff; and have punitive teachers (Gottfredson & Gottfredson, 1985). One study found punishment and lack of praise by classroom teachers to be main factors related to delinquent behavior (Farrington, 1987).

Resiliency: Overcoming Risk
The majority of children do well in life despite adversity and exposure to multiple risks (Hawkins, 1995; Bernard, 1993). Children who are able to thrive despite risks are said to be resilient (Hawkins, 1995; Bernard, 1995; Katz, 1995; Bushweller, 1995; Viadero, 1995; Brooks, 1994). Researchers have identified certain protective factors that, like barriers at the tops of cliffs, can help promote resilience and prevent negative outcomes.

General Protective Factors
Protective factors, like risk factors, can be located within individuals, families, communities, and schools. They apply to all children, including those who are disabled and otherwise at risk. The effects of these factors are cumulative—the more factors present, the greater their influence (Thornberry, 1994).

Individual Traits

Resilient children tend to have:

- Socially competent
- Autonomous
- Not easily frustrated
- Able to bounce back
- Not quick to give up
- Good natured
- Optimistic

- Intelligent
- Appealing to adults
- Able to elicit positive attention and support
- Good problem–solving skills
- A sense of purpose and personal control
- A future orientation
- High self–esteem

(Bernard, 1995; Hawkins, 1995; Sylwester, 1995; Brooks, 1994; Thornberry, 1994; Bernard, 1993)

Families/Communities

Families of resilient children exhibit:
- Warmth
- Affection
- Emotional support

(Brooks, 1994; Thornberry, 1994)

Children and parents or caretakers form mutual attachments, and children are monitored and supervised. Likewise, communities can nurture, monitor, supervise, and convey prosocial values to children.

Schools

Schools that have the most success with ODD and disruptive students:

- Convey compassion, understanding, respect
- Show an interest for children and families
- Present opportunities for meaningful participation
- Identify children's strengths and talents
- Organize learning accordingly

- Incorporate learning styles
- Consider multiple intelligences
- Use an accelerated, rich curriculum that includes art, music, and athletics
- Design classroom instruction to accommodate various ability levels and maximize learning time

(Bernard, 1995; Bushweller, 1995; Katz, 1995; Viadero, 1995)

Research shows that school organization—management, governance, culture, and climate—can reduce overall measures of student disruption as effectively as individual treatment programs (Gottfredson, 1987; Gottfredson, 1984). Through cooperation and collaboration, schools can draw on internal and community resources to meet students' needs. Other school–related, protective factors include boosting achievement in mathematics and reading (especially 4th-grade reading scores), commitment to school, and attachment to teachers (Bernard, 1995, Bushweller, 1995; Shaw, 1992).

STRATEGY #45

A Model for Promoting Prosocial Behavior

Perhaps the most critical factor influencing the development of prosocial behavior is attachment to at least one prosocial adult who believes in the child and provides unconditional acceptance and support (Hawkins, 1995; 1994; Brooks, 1994; Bernard, 1995; Katz, 1995). Hawkins explains that prosocial behavior results when children bond with prosocial adults and peers and adopt their beliefs and values (Hawkins, 1995). Conversely, antisocial behavior results if children bond to antisocial individuals, such as gang members, and adopt their beliefs and values instead.

For bonding to occur, three conditions must be present:
- An opportunity for bonding to take place
- Cognitive and social skills to help children succeed in bonding opportunities
- A consistent system of recognition and reinforcement for accomplishments

A resilient temperament, social competence, and cognitive skills are protective factors that help children participate successfully in prosocial bonding opportunities. Recognition reinforces what children are doing right, plus provides an incentive to persist in bonding activities and relationships.

Many experts agree that attachment to even one caring, responsible adult—whether a teacher, administrator, bus driver, custodian, relative, or community member—can help children become prosocial (Bernard, 1995; Hawkins, 1995; Katz, 1995; Brooks, 1994). A study of the effects of remediation on delinquency showed that the child's bond with the tutor affected school attitude and behavior more than improved grades (Keilitz & Dunivant, 1995).

The important role of bonding in the development of prosocial behavior offers schools an avenue for effective prevention and intervention. One-on-one mentoring programs can help children develop relationships that foster self–esteem, social attachment, and prosocial behavior (Bowman & Bowman, 1997).

Children seek to imitate and gain approval from their role models, whether good or bad. Once children bond with antisocial peer groups, their behavior becomes more difficult to change. Schools, families, and communities can work together to ensure that all children are cared for and have prosocial adults to emulate, thus assuring the transmission of prosocial beliefs and values to the next generation.

STRATEGY #46

Maximizing Opportunities for Bonding

If students are to form attachments to school and prosocial role models, then policies and practices should ensure that teachers, students, parents, and communities have the time and means to get to know each other. For example, policy actions might involve extending the school year or the school day, revising consolidation plans and class size limits, adding community service to graduation requirements, or creating a program to assign personal coaches or mentors for students with IEPs or recurring discipline referrals. Related school practices might include improving school attendance, looping (teachers and classes stay together for two or more years), block scheduling, teaming, cooperative learning, mentoring or coaching, and one-on-one tutoring (Bushweller, 1995; Chaskin & Rauner, 1995; Kohn, 1993).

Policies and practices that support prosocial bonding do not isolate and alienate children unnecessarily through tracking, special education placement, suspension, or expulsion, and do not encourage the formation of deviant peer groups by placing "problem" children together for instruction or discipline. Cooperative learning groups, conflict resolution and anger management training, group activities, and counseling help children to learn alternatives to antisocial behavior, to deal with their emotions, and to get along with others.

For Every Risk, Seek Protection

By identifying both risk factors and protective factors, research has given us the tools to build solutions—barriers at the tops of cliffs that keep children from falling—and has restored our hope that we, collectively and individually, can make a difference.

The Teflon™ Technique

Objectives: 1. The students will learn to respond versus react to others.
2. The students will write "I messages" to set boundaries with others.

Materials: Teflon™ skillet, paper, and pencil or pen

Motivation: Show the students a Teflon™ skillet. Ask what is special about a Teflon™ skillet. (Elicit that food does not stick very easily to it when cooked.) Explain how you hope they will be "Teflon™ kids" who know how to handle annoying, aggravating behaviors of others.

Lesson: 1. Have students share their "pet peeves" that others do to them. List these on the board.

2. Explain that while annoying behaviors are a part of life, it is to their advantage to know how to respond in such a way to reduce the annoyance as much as possible. Teach students that there are two things they can do to be "Teflon™ kids": "disengage" and give "I messages."

3. Teach students how to "disengage." Disengage means to refuse to get in the middle of a bad situation. Instead of arguing or getting upset, a person can consciously make a decision to ignore the behavior or walk away. Explain that we give the person who is aggravating us a lot of power when we get upset. But when we disengage, the negative things that others say or do "slide" right on past and don't stick.

4. Teach assertiveness skills by using "I messages." Use the following example: "I feel frustrated when you make noises in class. Please go elsewhere to do that."

   The three steps of an "I message" are:
   (1) Share a feeling: e.g., "I feel frustrated…"
   (2) Explain why: e.g., "…when you make noises in class"
   (3) Make a request: e.g., "Please go elsewhere to do that."

5. Have students visualize at least three irritating situations and write down their "I messages" in response.

6. Have volunteers role play some of their responses using the "I messages" they have written.

Application: Ask students to keep a journal for the next two or three days recording how they were like "Teflon™" when aggravating situations arose.

Control Card

Objective: Students will learn a model for reducing impulsive behaviors.

Materials: 3" X 5" index card
colored markers

Motivation: Ask "What is the difference between a foolish person and a wise person?"

Lead students to understand that the difference involves how much the brain is used. Wise people think before they act.

Lesson: Tell the students that today they will be making a tool that can greatly help them to make wise choices. This tool is called a "control card."

Pass out 3" X 5" index cards and ask students to copy down the following three questions:

- What am I getting ready to do?
- What will happen if I do this?
- What could I do instead?

Have students memorize the three questions to ask themselves to control impulsive behaviors. Allow students time to quiz each other.

Ask students to decorate their "control cards" with colored markers. Have students write "Control Card" on the opposite side from the three questions that they have already written.

Application: Carry the "Control Card" in a pocket or put it in a visible spot as a constant reminder to stop and think before doing anything. Ask students to get into a conscious habit of using the three questions as a mental checklist before making decisions.

Chapter 3

Second Step: Moderate Interventions

The focus of this chapter involves interventions that are beyond prevention. In Chapter 2, the intent was to become aware of many of the dynamics that create, increase, or reinforce oppositional and defiant behaviors. In this chapter, the undesirable behaviors are there; we simply hope not to make matters worse and perhaps to lower the intensity a bit.

ODD and the Family:
Common Emotional and Behavioral Patterns

Children diagnosed with ODD are more likely to come from families whose members have been previously diagnosed with other psychiatric disorders such as depression/mood disorders, antisocial personality disorder, or a history of substance abuse. The presence of previously diagnosed psychiatric disorders in the family will obviously make treatment a considerable challenge. Yet to attempt to focus the treatment solely on the child and ignore the need for family involvement is a mistake. All members of the family need to be involved in treatment when a child has a behavior disorder. Simply put, the family will need to work together.

There is little doubt that families have a tremendous influence on a child's behavior both through socialization and genetics. One risk factor that increases the likelihood of developing oppositional defiant disorder is having parents with marginal, inconsistent discipline practices (Frick, et al., 1991). Prior research also suggests parental rejection and coercion to be associated with oppositional and defiant problems (Dishion, et al., 1991; Webster-Stratton, 1989). It's also important to keep in mind that socioeconomic status may play a role in ODD and CD. Green et al. (2002) reported that children diagnosed as ODD had significantly lower socioeconomic status (SES) than psychiatric comparison subjects and that the SES of children diagnosed with both ODD and CD was significantly lower than that of those subjects diagnosed with ODD alone.

Research also suggests that a high level of parent stress places a child at risk for developing ODD (Webster-Stratton, 1989). This research indicated that mothers of children who are oppositional and defiant are at increased risk for marital stress. Subjects in these studies also reported that they were dissatisfied with their marital relationships. When mothers have low marital satisfaction, they are more likely to have negative perceptions of their children and to make unrealistic and poorly executed requests of them. This same research reported that mothers with low marital satisfaction were also more likely to discipline harshly and inconsistently (Stoneman, et al., 1989).

Helping the Entire Family

It should be clear from the descriptors listed above that effective treatment always involves changes within the family system. Research has demonstrated the efficacy of a particular model of family treatment known as Parent Management Training (PMT), which is a system that teaches parents to manage their child's behavioral problems in the home and at school. In PMT, parent-child interactions are modified in ways that are designed to promote pro-social, compliant behavior and to decrease antisocial or oppositional behavior. Initially, parents are trained to have periods of positive play interaction with their child. They then receive further training to identify the child's positive behaviors and to reinforce these behaviors. In effect, parents are trained to "catch the child being good." At that point, parents are trained in the use of brief negative consequences for misbehavior. Treatment sessions provide the parents with opportunities to practice and refine the techniques. Randomized controlled trials have found that PMT is more effective in changing antisocial behavior and promoting pro-social behavior than many other commonly used treatments (e.g., relationship, play therapy, family therapies, varied community services) and control conditions (e.g., waiting-list, "attention-placebo") (Feldman & Kadzin, 1995).

There isn't a cure for ODD. While certain medications may help control some of the symptoms that occur with the comorbid disorders, there isn't a drug that will negate the behaviors associated with ODD. Children diagnosed with ADHD may take stimulant medication to improve their focus. Depressed children are often prescribed medication to enhance their mood. There is no such drug with ODD. The best treatment approach involves families that help themselves by making some changes that will help manage the child's behavior.

One of the most important things to do is improve communication within the family and between all parties that have contact with the child. ODD is often associated with "playing both ends against the middle." Children with ODD frequently assume the role of the victim by describing the ways their parents, teachers, or principals are mistreating them. The only way to put a stop to this is for all stakeholders to communicate on a frequent basis.

The family needs to have a behavior management plan. Children with ODD are good at creating confusion; and unless there is a well-conceived plan, they will find the weak points in the arrangements and exploit them. The plan needs to be specific. Any plan that is too general will bring up points of contention between parents and the child. Plans that contain statements such as, "Mike will behave" or "Mike will act appropriately" are doomed to fail. What exactly do the parents mean by terms like "behave" and "appropriately?" Parents need to remain calm when enforcing the plan. Emotions need to be held in check because too much emotion leads to poor decision making. Readers are encouraged to learn more about the PMT model described above which can be of assistance in the development and management of the behavior management plan.

Last but not least, the family needs support. A support group sponsored by a mental health clinic is an excellent idea to provide opportunities to discuss the trials and tribulations of raising a child with a behavioral disorder. Parents need to know they are not alone. Having the opportunity to share experiences and also brainstorm workable solutions can prove to be of significant benefit to parents of ODD children.

Medications

There is no one medication that can be prescribed for ODD. Depending on the individual characteristics and etiology of a student's behaviors and emotions, there may be medications that effectively address some issues. If you have determined that the student you are concerned with is moderately to severely impacted by ODD characteristics, you may want to seek a medical assessment to determine if the student might benefit from one or more medications.

A quick note of caution: Unless you have a medical degree, you should avoid recommending that a student needs medication. The more appropriate direction to take in a discussion is to help the child's parents understand the severity of the difficulties (no doubt they probably have insight from situations at home and in the community) and suggest that additional professional guidance might be useful. Most parents will naturally consider taking their child to a medical doctor for assessment.

Provide Antidotes for Medication Saboteurs

Medication may sometimes be a useful part of the overall plan for a student with ODD. However, the use of medication can easily be sabotaged. ODD students are more likely than most students to see medication as one more attempt of the adult world to control them. Oppositional students may be easily embarrassed and may refuse to come to receive medications if others are watching. ODD students are always inclined to pit the family against the school, and the issue of medications can become a very strong tool for divisiveness.

Provide antidotes to these and other saboteurs by:

• Respecting privacy when managing medications.
• Avoid granting magical power to a medication by attributing either the occurrence or the absence of a behavior to it.
• Educating the student about his or her medication.
• Encouraging the student to self-monitor the effects of medications.

Provide Accurate Feedback to Medical Personnel Regarding Medications

Medications can have an impact on every aspect of school behavior, including task completion, peer relationships, responsiveness to directives, operating under a timeline, remaining in a location, and overall behavior. School personnel need to have an ongoing communication with medical personnel who prescribe and monitor medications. The following form is suggested as one method to maintain this dialogue.

MEDICAL SUPPORT INFORMATION EXCHANGE FORM

This form provides a means of exchanging information between staff members who provide daily supervision and structure for the student/client and medical personnel who are providing intervention through medication.

Parental permission to share information:

Parent signature: _____ Date: _____

Student: _____

School/Service Provider: _____

Information provided by School/Service Provider:

Staff member providing information: _____

Phone #: _____ Best time to call: _____

Behavioral/academic/mental health concerns:

Questions/comments concerning medication:

Other comments:

Information provided by medical staff:

Staff member providing information: _____

Phone #: _____ Best time to call: _____

Behavioral/academic/mental health concerns:

Questions/comments concerning medication:

Other comments:

STRATEGY #53

Medication Ownership

For some students the roots of their oppositional behavior are in their temperament, or tied to biochemical issues. Medication may sometimes be helpful. It is critical for the student to feel as responsible as possible regarding the medication. If you overtly use it as a means of controlling the student, the student is likely to sabotage its effectiveness. Try to involve the student in assessing the medication for benefits that he or she wants. Always emphasize that the medication is a tool that may benefit the student.

STRATEGY #54

Share Medication Information Resources with Parents and Students

It is impossible to keep up with the constant evolution in medications. The best source of up-to-date information on specific medications is the Web. However, there are a number of common questions and concerns that parents, students, and sometimes staff members have. Some excellent resources to have on hand and share are:

It's Nobody's Fault – New Hope and Help for Difficult Children
By Harold S. Koplewicz, M.D.

Straight Talk About Psychiatric Medications for Kids
By Timothy E. Wilens, M.D.

Additional references may provide basic information regarding medications. The following reference books are excellent sources of information. Note that these sources are routinely updated.

2005 Physicians' Desk Reference
Publisher: Thompson PDR

PDR Drug Guide for Mental Health Professionals, 2nd Edition
Publisher: Thompson PDR

Advances in medications occur at a rapid pace. You may want to consult websites for the most current information regarding medications.

Practice Patience with your Payoffs

The ODD student will rarely respond to either your punishments or your rewards with, "Thank you so much for the powerful lesson…I shall be forever changed by your brilliant behavior management skills!" More likely, the student will choose to not respond as predicted unless and until it is clear that you are not too concerned about the student's choice. Remember, "When you punish or reward me, I feel that you are trying to control or manipulate me."

Many ODD students will simply resist obvious management strategies simply because she/he is ODD! When the authority figure does excellent management work, i.e., is clear, brief, and consistent, the ODD student has a well-defined target of resistance. You may view this as clearly "drawing the line in the sand." The ODD student is likely to say, "Thanks for letting me know where the line is so that I can clearly step over it."

For these reasons it is so important to be calm, rational, and smart about planning your strategies. You do not want to be planning at a moment of emotion. Once you have your plan, implement it, stay on course, and understand that the student is probably going to resist your plan. When the student finally comes around and begins to adhere to your expectations, continue to remain calm. Any perception that you "won" will draw an immediate effort at proving you wrong!

Reframing for Positive Expectations: Finding Lemonade in Lemons

It is easy to get caught up in seeing the things wrong with an ODD student. We will develop our "list" of objectionable characteristics about the student and have the list ready for instant confirmation. This causes us to expect the worst and to respond in ways that encourage the student to continue in their negative behavior patterns.

"Reframing" is the art of looking carefully at the behavior descriptors and finding something positive buried within the negative. For example, instead of saying that a student is "bossy," view the student as a good organizer who likes to offer leadership. You may laugh, but since communication experts tell us that around 85% of our communication is non-verbal, it is important to begin to see things differently. When you change your thoughts, you will find it easier to change your nonverbal behaviors.

Following are some suggestions that might fit some of your ODD students.

STANDARD TERMINOLOGY	REFRAMED
Loses temper	Passionate; having deep convictions
Argumentative	Active, not apathetic; sees alternative perspectives
Defiant	Assertive; independent; a leader, not a follower
Annoying	Persistent
Blaming	Reflective; courage to confront
Touchy	Sensitive
Angry and resentful	Having the courage to stand up; has a good memory
Spiteful and vindictive	A critical analyzer; having a persistent sense of justice

Challenging students come in many flavors. The chart above provides a few ideas specific to the eight diagnostic criteria of oppositional and defiant children and youth. No doubt you will need to practice this strategy with many students and with many negative labels and phrases. The following page offers a worksheet that will be useful in this process.

Reframing:
There are Silver Linings in these Clouds

Reframing is not natural; it begins with honest thoughts and feelings.
In order to train yourself to do the un-natural, follow these steps.

Allow yourself to let the negative thoughts and feelings flow.
What do you believe are some of the negative characteristics of the student?

_____

_____

Spend some creative time re-labeling each of the negative characteristics with more positive labels. You will need to stretch a bit. You may want to think with a large dose of humor:

_____

_____

Plan to begin using the more positive labels. Your plan may include several components.
Changing behavior, including your own, is difficult!

1. You will need to explain your reframing strategy to other adults who will hear your new terminology.
You will need to solicit their participation in the reframing. Who do you need to bring on board?

_____

_____

2. You will need to plan prompts for yourself (as will the other adults).
    Suggestions include notes in significant places and rehearsals.
    Reframing must be done with a straight face. What prompts will you use?

_____

_____

Create New Myths

Everyone lives with a number of "myths" that affect decision-making and behavior. For example, an early experience of tripping and falling down a couple of times may cause those around you to label you as "clumsy." This label may begin to affect your self-expectations, such that for years you view yourself as clumsy. Whenever you fall, trip, or drop something, you may hear that inside voice echoing the label…And you may find yourself avoiding situations that you perceive of as requiring "non-clumsy" skills.

ODD children suffer from expectation myths also. You can contribute to others in your school changing their "myths" of the ODD student by sharing your reframing comments and observations about the student. If your co-workers hear about "Danny's attention to detail," they may develop this more positive way of viewing what was previously identified as "argumentative."

Careful Communication

Careful communication involves effectively using your body, mind, and mouth in such a way as to reduce anger and conflict. When an angry, aggressive youth is acting in a hostile way, remember the following tips. Keep in mind that in a normal situation, people listen and respond rationally. However, in an anxiety producing situation, the upset party keys into paraverbals and nonverbals. Therefore, the adult in charge has to think about how he or she is coming across to the already upset person in terms of body language and verbal expression.

Body (Watch your nonverbals)
- Personal space allowance (stand about three feet away)
- Nonthreatening posture (stand sideways in relation to the upset person)
- Eye contact (without staring, look at the person who is talking)
- Relaxed facial expressions
- Head nods (simply acknowledge that you hear what the other person is saying)

Mind
- Concentrate on what is being said
- Try to understand the child or teen's point of view
  (You don't have to agree with what is said; just listen!)
- Avoid interrupting and jumping to conclusions

Mouth
- Use facilitative responses
- Reflect the child or teen's feelings
- Summarize and clarify what is being said
- Ask open questions to get the facts (what, when, where, and how)

Personal Prescription

The teacher and student agree upon a goal or two each morning. The goal(s) is/are written in the form of a closed question. At the end of the day, the teacher and student determine if the goal(s) was/were met and reward accordingly. In this way, bite-sized specific goals are being addressed, and the student with ODD is not overwhelmed by trying to fix every problematic behavior at once. A "snow-balling" effect begins to occur as small, attainable target behaviors are met. Other behaviors improve with the student's increased efforts and successes.

Example:

Name: <u>Joe D'fiant</u>
      1. Did I follow directions?
      2. Did I complete assigned work?

Power Struggles

We have all been in them, and usually we don't plan them. There is usually verbal escalation, on both individual's parts, and very little listening. More often than not, there is an audience. And both individuals are focused on defeating the opponent. The power struggle is made for ODD students! They are masters at trapping the authority in this activity.

Avoid Behaviors that Add to the Power Struggle:

- Trying to convince
- Threatening
- Increasing the consequences as the discussion continues
- Having the interaction in front of others
- Responding emotionally (getting angry or frustrated)
- Bringing up other issues

STRATEGY #61

Use Behaviors that Diminish Power Struggles:

- Privacy
- Listening
- Simple directives and choices

- Brief comments
- Walking away
- Saying, "I want you to have the last word"

STRATEGY #62

The Pitfall of Excessive Persuasion

Be careful with talking too much. While your goal may be to help the ODD student gain insight and new skills, the ODD student may perceive of your talking as a potential mine field in which to get you to blow up. The more you say, the more the student has to argue about or to trip you up. While we may feel that "if the student just hears what I need to say, it will finally help him/her realize the error of his/her ways," the student probably is receiving the words as grounds for an argument.

STRATEGY #63

Give Me a Chance to Think About What You Have Said

This strategy buys a little "calm down" time. When things are getting heated, you may state that you need time to think about the points the student is making. Or, you may state that you know these issues are important to the student, and all the distractions of that moment in the class make it difficult for you to devote your full and undivided attention to the student's issue. Tell the student to drop by your classroom after school and you will have an answer. By that time the student may have lost emotional steam. Also, the interaction will not be in the presence of an audience.

Avoid Participating in ODD as a Sporting Event

As they do in a power struggle, ODD students would choose to view all interactions in terms of win/lose. The ODD student is very competitive and will be creative in their attempts to gain "victory." Resolve that this is not a win/lose sporting event. As often as possible do not allow yourself to be the opponent. Do not take things personally. Do not look for vengeance. Set expectations up in an impersonal way: "...the rules say," or "...the clock says." Make sure that all expectations are clear up front. Follow through. Be calm and businesslike.

Discovering the Cool Spot

We are familiar with the concept of the "hot spot." You know—that one little thing that will set you off in an irrational frenzy. Sometimes we overlook the cool spots. A cool spot is a word or phrase that immediately calms you or gets you to refocus. Tune in to words, phrases, issues, or ideas that your "problem child" responds to in a positive way. For example, you may find out that the student is quite skilled at handling the classroom computer. Out of the presence of others (to avoid the ODD student having to appear as though they like your praise...) calmly praise the student about their special talent or interest, or express interest in the area, or ask for help from the student. You may find that tapping into this area of interest or expertise will "buy you time" or distract the student from their otherwise oppositional behavior.

Be Narrow-minded

ODD students may provoke you to seeing too much. If you try to eliminate all negative behaviors at once you will not succeed. Pick one behavior that you wish to focus on. You may want to pick the easiest behavior to work on. Carefully count the behavior—how often does it occur? When does it occur? If you are able to reduce the number of incidences and/or the number of times it occurs, you have found success. Narrow your focus!

Private Interactions

ODD students will go out of their way to save face. As often as possible try to have brief private interactions to avoid the complication of the ODD student needing to show others that he/she is still in charge. You may ask the student to run an errand, then intercept the student before he or she re-enters the classroom. Or, if you routinely roam around your classroom, you are able to interact privately with most students. That way, no one knows what you are saying to the ODD student.

STRATEGY #68

Be Direct and Show Your Briefs

When you give a directive, make it brief and direct. The more time you spend explaining, the more likely the ODD student sees your explanation as an opportunity to wiggle out of something. State your directive, then move on. Do not wait for the student to respond or agree. Time is on your side more than you might think. When you walk away, the student may view that as "decision-making" time. Just the notion of having that power sometimes works in your favor.

For example, the students in your class are working on an in-class assignment. "Bob," your challenging student, is dawdling towards completion. He often complains that you have not given him enough time, and that your teaching skills are highly suspect.

As you move about the classroom in your style of never staying stuck in one place behind your desk, you walk past a number of students, making brief comments. As you pass by Bob, you state, "The papers are to be in the basket at 11:00." You barely slow down to make the statement, and you continue to move past Bob immediately after the statement. If, instead, you had chosen to stop and remind Bob of his usual difficulty in completing assignments on time, you probably would have set up an opportunity for resistance. State it briefly. Move on.

STRATEGY #69

Impersonal Interactions

The ODD child has a drive to oppose you. Remove yourself from the equation. Attribute your directive to something outside of yourself:

For example, you know that language arts class begins in seven minutes, and you need to prompt the students to complete their current math assignment, prepare to put away the math book, and get the reading book. Instead of saying, "I want you to get ready for language arts," say "The clock says that it is almost time for language arts." Instead of having you to say "no" to, the student is faced with the impersonal clock. State your message and move on. Do not fall into the trap of letting the ODD child make it personal.

STRATEGY #70

State, do not Ask

If you use a question format when you give a command, what do you expect the ODD student to do!?! For example, "John, would you like to work on your math now?" "No." Avoid this request format. As you choose your words and phrases, always keep in mind the motivations that are at work in the ODD student—to oppose, to frustrate, to trump your power.

STRATEGY #71

Honesty is the Best Policy

ODD students are innately distrusting of the intentions of others. To establish and maintain credibility, it is important to be honest with the student. Do not try to manipulate or trick them into doing something. Be very direct and identify the benefit for both the student and yourself.

Take the situation near the end of a semester when grades are due to be posted. Your administrator has given a deadline by which time you must turn in grades. You know how long it takes you to complete computations of grades, so you know when you need all assignments that will go into grading to be completed. You say to the students, "I will be turning in grades Wednesday afternoon. In order to do so, no assignments will be accepted after 4 p.m. Monday to allow me time to do my work." It is clear from this statement that your deadline is based on your need for time to do the work. There are no hidden agendas.

Attitudinal Therapy

This package of techniques may work with some ODD students, while others will respond by rejecting your positiveness. The basics of attitudinal therapy call for you to be neutral and businesslike when the student is being negative, and for you to be positive and engaging when the student is neutral to positive in their behaviors. The caution is that some ODD students respond to excessive positiveness by feeling that you are trying to manipulate them, and they actively rebel against this manipulation. If this occurs, remain neutral at all times, even during the positive behaviors.

Discretion is Better than Valor

So, you have determined that the student gets worse when you show positive feelings about his or her behavior. And then the student acts worse, so you have concluded that you must remain neutral, even when the student is being positive. Bummer! But there is another subtlety to keep in mind—You may need to discreetly and neutrally state your satisfaction. For some ODD students the teacher's positive regard is important, though the student's outward behavior may not indicate this. For these students, a neutral tone, with the positive regard calmly and privately stated, is received and appreciated.

STRATEGY #74

An Argument for Rational Discipline Behaviors

Most of us have habits, or patterns of behavior, for responding to events. When we are under pressure, feeling challenged, or dealing with resistance, there are three general response styles:

- *Fight* - We respond actively, defending our position and attacking the resistance. An example would be demanding that an unruly student leave your classroom immediately and never return. Fight responses often lead to additional conflicts and power struggles as each party attempts to gain the upper hand.

- *Flight* - We respond by becoming passive and/or attempting to leave the situation. In schools an example would be calling in sick to avoid dealing with a difficult class. Flight responses may lead to a sense of being victimized, appearing powerless, and encouraging additional resistance.

- *Rational* - We respond by implementing plans or actions that were previously determined or established in a logical, predictable way. An example would be following through on consequences with consistency and a matter-of-fact calm demeanor. Rational responses may provide the consistency of learning experiences that allows a student to learn from his/her experiences. Also, rational responses may help the staff members feel more in control, as they will be in control of their own behavior.

The following situations illustrate examples of each response style. Review these examples and see which response would most closely match your own.

Situation One

John, who is chronically late to your class, comes in after the bell rings and walks slowly to his desk, talking to other students as he enters. You:

Response 1.   With a tone of anger and exasperation you call out to John as he reaches his desk that you are sick and tired of his know-it-all attitude and that you will be forced to report him to the principal for his disruptive behavior.

Response 2.   Realizing that this will only continue to happen if you make a big deal out of it, you choose to ignore the behavior.

Response 3.   You quietly walk over to John a couple of minutes after he enters and ask him to see you after class. Your plan is to remind him that if he accumulates five tardies, he will be required to stay after school for work detail and that he already has four.

Situation Two

Once again Sally and Wanda got into a fight during lunch break. You only get 15 minutes for lunch, and you are furious that you have to use it to intervene with their conflict. This is the second time this week this has happened. You:

Response 1.   Angrily shout at the students that they just can't seem to get along for 15 measly minutes and that you are going to get to the bottom of this right now. You grab Sally by the arm and march her off to the office, demanding that Wanda follow.

Response 2.   You decide that this is simply going to continue, so you write a note to the principal requesting that one of the students be changed to another class so that their lunch schedules do not coincide.

Response 3.   You ask another staff member to back you up as you firmly instruct the students to follow you to the office. Once in the office you provide guidelines for the discussion, and give each student an opportunity to tell what happened. After a brief discussion aimed at helping the students discover ways to manage their conflict more appropriately, you remind the students that the consequence of a second fight is after-school detention for five days. Though the students protest and attempt to convince you to change the detention to three days "for trying to solve our problem," you hold your ground and calmly, but directly, state that you expect to see them after school in the detention room.

Situation Three

It is the third week of class, and most of your students have settled into an acceptable routine. Larry, however, continues to be disrespectful and rude, often mumbling what you suspect are obscenities under his breath whenever you give him a directive. It is Monday afternoon, and Larry has been particularly irritating all day. As you dismiss the class, you remind them of their homework assignments. Larry says, "Screw you and your homework assignment," and throws his worksheet on the floor. You:

Response 1.   Blow up. Larry has finally stepped on your last nerve. You yell at him to immediately sit in his chair as the other students leave. Some are laughing, and this really gets you fired up. You take their names down and state that you will deal with them tomorrow. Meanwhile Larry begins to wander around the room, daring you to make him sit down.

Response 2.   Think to yourself, "Larry is only hurting himself; if I confront him there is no telling what he will do. I will just let this slide and refer him to the psychologist for evaluation."

Response 3. [...] e other students for a good day, and move toward the door to say [...] e as they leave. Larry moves your way as you position yourself near [...], but not blocking his exit to the door. You say to Larry, "I've been [...] about you; is something bothering you?" Larry looks down and [...] les, "It's none of your business." After the other students are gone, you [...] to Larry that you will be glad to give him extra help, but that the [...] ework is required and that not doing it will result in a zero for that grade. [...] ther you remind Larry that speaking to the teacher in such a disrespectful [...] y will result in lunch detention for the next day. Larry states that he doesn't [...] are and that you cannot make him stay in. You remind Larry that if he does [...] not stay in for lunch detention, the rules require a parent conference and [...] after-school detention.

[...] parent that the more desirable response in each of these scenarios is #3. The style depicted [...] #1 reflects the "fight" response. While you may overpower the student (physically or with the authority of your position) and force things to go your way, it is likely that the student will be embarrassed, feel the need to save face, and quietly desire or plan a way to get back at you in the future. Response #2 illustrates a "flight" response. Resistant students are likely to "up the ante" to see where your limits really are. Other students may join in actively or passively, testing your control and influence in the classroom. Response #3 is the **rational** style. Several elements of this style are evident: the teacher remains calm, but is directive. There is a sense of measured response. Consequences are pre-determined and followed up on. Words are carefully chosen to support the notion that the student is making choices that have understood consequences. The teacher is careful to avoid "fighting words," or words that bait the student for an argument. On the other hand, the teacher avoids being drawn into a verbal fight, or being distracted from the main issue and the follow-up of consequences. It is our contention that being rational allows you to remain in control, regardless of how the student responds. Being rational helps students realize that they are responsible for the consequences of their own behavior choices. Finally, being rational helps one maintain a lower stress perspective on the responsibilities of teaching.

On the following page we have a review sheet that may be useful as you analyze your management experiences with challenging students.

Reflecting for the Rational Response
FIGHT VS. FLIGHT VS. RATIONAL

The purpose of this reflection form is to structure a review of the approach you take in events that require management and discipline actions.

Briefly describe the event that required action. _____

_____

_____

How did you handle the situation? _____

_____

_____

In the above response, identify and label anything you did that you might describe as using the "fighting" approach, the "flight" approach, or the "rational" approach.

We tend to respond with either a fight or a flight (move away from) approach to situations that feel threatening. The threat may be to our identities, our thoughts, our feelings, or our physical selves. If you used a "fight or flight" approach, try to identify and put into words your sense of feeling threatened.

_____

_____

_____

How could you manage the threatening feelings? Is it possible to change your thoughts or interpretations of the events so that you do not focus on or interpret the event as threatening?

_____

_____

What will you do the next time, and how will you train and prompt yourself to follow through?

_____

_____

The Elimination Errand

If you anticipate a resistant behavior, send the student on an errand to the office. Make it a habit to use students to run errands so that you may speak in an ODD avoidance when you need to. And remember, timing is important. Also, you may want to time things so that you secretly meet the student in the hall, out of the view of other students, as the student returns. You might find a moment of privacy for any necessary discussion.

Consider this example. Tom has been one of your students for three months. You know his patterns, and you know that he will consistently move from a sullen look to a verbal refusal to a resistant explosion. In your class, you frequently ask students to run an in-school errand, so when you see Tom beginning to get that scowl, you ask him to take an envelope to the office. Before he returns to the class, you step into the hall and speak to him briefly and privately. You step back into class, allowing Tom to walk in a moment later.

Embrace the Student's Feelings

The ODD student thrives on arguing. You may want to occasionally respond to an argument by stating, "This seems really important to you. Instead of finishing our talk in class, we will talk in private after class." You have validated the student, and chances are slim that he or she will actually show up after class.

This is My Story and I am Sticking To It

Remind yourself what to expect about ODD students:
- **They are resistant to learning from consequences**
- **They suspect that you are trying to control them, so they resist compliance**
- **They will never thank you for your brilliant and effective strategies**

So *when you are clear-minded*, develop your plan and stick to it. An observation: I have never experienced any student, particularly an ODD student, saying, "Thank you so much for your effective work at changing my behavior…I am forever changed with your behavioral brilliance!" Finally, remember that a student's failure to comply does not mean that you have failed or that your plan is a bad one!

The Confusion about Reinforcement

ODD students have trouble accepting reinforcement attempts, as they are bound and determined to avoid being "controlled" by you! So keep in mind that your reinforcement may have to be given discreetly to avoid other students' awareness. Also, remember that you may have to stay calm and not show much emotion when a student does comply and receive a reinforcement.

For example, you have noticed that when you praise Amanda in class, it always results in her disagreeing and eventually walking out of class. She may be sensitive to her peers watching the reinforcement, a.k.a., "manipulation," going on and have to resist it. Instead, you make a plan to discreetly place a sticky note on her desk.

Psychological Martial Arts

Argumentative, belligerent behaviors come with the territory of oppositional defiant disorder. The responses by adults will either diffuse or inflame the situation. The following four steps help those in authority to work with the child rather than giving the impression of working against him or her. The key to these steps involves the "facilitative responses."

To get the best responses from people, try:
1. Using feeling-focused responses (reflect the feelings of the person)
   "I can tell you are very frustrated right now."
2. Summarizing and clarifying what the person is saying.
   "So you think the teacher's decision is unreasonable."
3. Asking open-ended questions.
   (Use what, when, where and how questions. Avoid why questions.)
   "Tell me again, what exactly happened?"

How to Handle a Verbal "Attack"

1. Find out where your opponent's "attack" is coming from. Use open-ended questions such as "What" and "How" to explore his or her story and beliefs about the situation. Avoid asking "Why" questions because they may sound blaming.

2. Study your opponent's power. Use feeling-focused responses to study your opponent's emotions about the situation.

3. Grab hold of this power, step out of its way, and encourage it to move past you without letting it get to you. Use summarizing responses to keep the focus away from you for a while. This may help diffuse his or her "attack" and help you keep "cool."

4. If this fails, walk away without saying another word. If you can't walk away, "keep your cool" until you can talk it out with a support person.

(From Bowman, R. (1989) Motivating At-Risk Children. Workshop booklet. Developmental Resources, Inc.)

PANS room

PANS is an acronym for Plan A New Start. When kids misbehave, they often need more than a time out. The PANS room is designed to help students accept responsibility for inappropriate behavior and to make a suitable plan in order to get back to class. In essence, the student has to negotiate his or her way back into the classroom.

The PANS room differs greatly from In School Suspension (ISS) in two key ways. First, the student in large part can control how long he or she stays in the PANS room. Once appropriate behavior is displayed and an acceptable plan is written, the student is able to return to class. Secondly, a behavior teacher who manages the PANS room works with the student to discuss the situation and help formulate the behavior plan. This is a teaching situation where the behavior teacher actively helps the student learn information and skills to improve behavior.

Follow-up

1. Once a behavior plan is developed, it is distributed to every person on staff who regularly comes in contact with the student. These staff members hold the student accountable to follow through on the plan. If the student does not follow the plan, he or she returns to the PANS room.

2. The behavior teacher follows up with each student who has been to the PANS room. He or she observes the student's behavior periodically and has one-to-one conferences to discuss what progress has been made.

Two Main Rules

Two rules are stressed throughout the school year. They are:

1. You cannot keep others from learning.

2. You cannot violate the rights of others.

These rules are reviewed with the students on a regular basis. When they are broken in a severe way or on a chronic basis, the misbehaving student is escorted to the PANS room by a person on staff.

The Behavior Teacher

The behavior teacher needs to be an effective blend between a caring adult and a person who means business. A firm but fair approach is needed. The goal here is not to lecture and yell at misbehaving students. Instead the goal is to ask the hard questions to get the student to take responsibility and to get the student to commit to making a plan of action for improved behavior. Conversely, the student doesn't need a soft approach either. Only when the student is sincerely making an effort to get back on track should he or she be allowed to go back to class.

It is recommended that the person manning the PANS room have teaching experience so he or she can understand both the teacher's and student's point of view. Also recommended is a background in psychology and behavior management.

Developing a Plan

As a guideline for students making a plan to get back on track, these three questions could be utilized among others.

1. What is it that you really want to accomplish here at school?
   (Focus on positive goals related to school.)

2. What did you do that caused you to be sent down to the PANS room?
   (The student needs to take responsibility for his or her actions.)

3. What are two or three positive things you are willing to do in order to reach your goals?
   (The student lists some positive behaviors to replace the negative ones that got him or her into trouble.)

For younger kids or kids with learning disabilities, the behavior teacher may need to physically write the plan. However, the ideas need to come from the student. Also, note that if the student is not ready to work on a plan or is still displaying negative behaviors, he or she simply stays in the PANS room as long as needed.

PANS room Protocol

When a student arrives in the PANS room, he or she has two options. The student can sit quietly and think or keep up with academic work, which is sent down by the teacher(s) as soon as possible. The student sits in a cubicle or study carrel. When it appears that the student is calm and collected, he or she is invited to negotiate a plan to get back into class.

A Caution

This program needs to be one that everyone on staff "buys into." Problems sometimes arise when a teacher feels a student hasn't been "punished enough." It could be that a student who works hard to correct behavior and writes a suitable behavior plan could get back to class in half an hour or so. If the teacher is still upset about the original incident, this can sabotage the program when the student returns. A sarcastic comment or facial expression can start the problem all over again. The teacher and student need to move forward trusting in good faith that the behavior problem has been resolved.

Walk-by Praise

ODD students often perceive praise as manipulation. When you praise them, they are likely to think, "oh no you don't" and respond by doing the opposite of what you would expect. Therefore it is useful to give quiet praise, without eye-contact, and without hanging around to see if the student likes the praise. Simply walk by and briefly state or give a non-verbal cue that the student's behavior is appropriate.

Puzzle Praise

This technique provides a nonverbal way to give a reward. Find something the student would work for. Either draw a picture of the item, or find a picture, and cut it into pieces. When the student does previously agreed upon target behaviors, quietly place a "puzzle piece" on the student's desk. When the student has acquired all of the puzzle pieces, they earn the prize. For example, a candy bar wrapper could be cut into pieces. When the student earns all of the pieces, he or she would receive the candy bar.

The Reinforcement Inventory

A "reinforcement" is a consequence (something that occurs after a behavior) that increases the likelihood that the behavior will occur more often or more intensely. A reinforcer may be either positive (something is given or gained), or negative (something is taken away). To determine what things or topics may be useful as reinforcers for your students, you may want to develop a questionnaire to find out what they are interested in. For ODD students, you should never label this questionnaire with any name that gives away your intention! Call it a "Subjects That are Interesting" list, or "Things that are Interesting," or "Things I know About" list. It helps if you solicit feedback from all of your students, not just those you are having difficulty with. This prevents the ODD student from gearing up to resist your request or anticipating that you may use the information to "manipulate" her or him.

STRATEGY #84

Home Rewards

Often there is a richer array of reinforcements available at home than at school. Parents may be willing to participate in contingencies between school and home. If the student completes some agreed upon task or behavior at school, then he/she would receive the reward available at home. A caution about this strategy is that ODD students are often in greater opposition at home than they are in at school. You would not choose this strategy unless you were confident that the parents would be in a position of participating consistently and effectively.

STRATEGY #85

Pair Positives and Negatives

When you are establishing contingencies for an ODD student, it is more effective to pair positive and negative outcomes. In other words, when the student does a specified behavior that you want, they earn a reward. When they do not do the behavior, not only do they not earn the reward, but they also lose something. For example, if the student completes his or her homework before dinnertime, he or she earns dessert. If the homework is not completed by dinnertime, the child does not get the dessert and does not get to watch TV.

STRATEGY #86

Deflecting the Blame: Avoiding Personal Responsibility

Since the student is actively looking for opportunities to oppose you, remove yourself as often as possible from the point of blame. Rely on "the rules," "the clock," or "the bell" when enforcing an expectation. For example, when a student is chewing gum, instead of saying "I told you not to chew gum," say "the rules say we cannot chew gum." The fight is not with you; it is with the rules.

The No Confidence Approach

As you begin to make a request of a student, interrupt yourself in mid-sentence, and state, "No, I don't think you are ready for this yet." If you are lucky, the ODD students will prove how wrong you are by quickly doing what you wanted them to do in the first place. Be sure to act a little annoyed that they proved you wrong.

STRATEGY #88

Enhancing Your Influence

Hopefully you have recognized that you are not able to control anyone else's behavior. Your goal should be to have maximum influence over your student's choices of behaviors. You gain influence by being consistent, predictable, and honest. State what you want and why you want it. Avoid behind-the-scenes manipulation. You also gain influence over time if the student begins to see that your advice pays off. The student will be motivated by doing what is good for himself or herself. Do not expect a student to do something "for you."

STRATEGY #89

How Can We Get Them Off of Your Back?

If you align yourself with the student by asking questions about what others have done to the student, you may be able to offer advice that the student perceives as helping him/her get others "off his/her back." You do not have to agree with the student, and you do not have to get into a position where you are making disparaging remarks about other staff members. (However, the student may perceive that you are agreeing with his/her negative assessment of other staff members; you may have to explain yourself to other staff at some point if they think that you have put them down to the student.) A bit of an irreverent attitude, showing some delight in the "plan," may help the student respond to your ideas. After all, one of the driving forces is to oppose others. If you are lucky, this opposition may take the form of the student proving to others that he or she is not as bad as they think!

You can also employ this strategy by finding another staff member who will approach the student with the idea of consulting with the student to get you off of his/her back. The student should not know that you really want this consultation to occur. The "consultant" can make it seem as though he/she is "playing the game" to get you off the student's case.

Instead of "ADHD," Focus on "Knowing Yourself"

Students feel out of control when adults focus the student's behavior as "due to ADHD." The student may reject this description and recoil at the suggestion of medications or other external controls. Instead of looking at the issue this way, consider having discussions where you talk about the differences in people. Ask the student, in non-judgmental terms, what they are like. Do they prefer to sit or move? To be outside or inside? To listen or do something? Help the student uncover personal strategies for maximizing their own control. Try to lead the student to the point of identifying what he/she needs to be successful.

Private Hand Signals

As often as possible use private communications with the ODD student. The more others observe your interactions, the more likely the student is to oppose you. ODD students would love to have a public challenge, so you should minimize the potential for that to happen. Previously agreed upon hand signals can be a useful way to communicate in a way that others do not see.

For example, you may develop a plan with an oppositional student so that when the student places his interlocked hands together and raises them over her or his head as in a stretching move, it means that he or she is not prepared to answer a question about the assignment. With this same student, you may work out a plan so that when you pull your earlobe, the student understands that signal to mean, "Get busy."

Self-Monitoring

When you are working on a specific behavior it is useful to have the student do their own frequency counts. Compare your count with the student. It is likely that the student will count less and generally disagree with your perceptions. There is no need to argue; benefit will be seen simply from having the student count. Listen to his or her explanations about why you are wrong. Nod your head and say, "I see," and move on. It is not necessary to reach agreement. In fact, the ODD student may prefer to feel that he or she has proven you wrong. The benefit of this technique is that the ODD student may develop greater self-awareness, and, in an effort to prove you wrong, actually reduce his or her inappropriate behaviors.

Know When to Hold 'Em and When to Fold 'Em

Borrowing from a well-known song, it is important to be able to stand firm on some issues—the non-negotiables—and to flex on others—the negotiables. This is particularly important for adolescents. One of the difficulties with adolescents who display oppositional behavior is that a certain amount of being oppositional is part of being an adolescent. Being able to negotiate is a skill that is appropriate for adolescents. The difficulty for the adult is knowing when you are dealing with normal adolescence and when you are dealing with unhealthy oppositional behavior. Since this will probably not be clear, it is important to decide prior to the interaction what is negotiable and what is not. A guideline to use is to let decisions based on family values be the non-negotiables. For example, a family value may be, "we do not hurt each other in this family." A negotiable might be the curfew set for weekends.

Retreat When Necessary

With adolescents it is important for everyone to agree on the principle of the retreat. Each person reserves the right to retreat for a time-out period to allow cooling off. Without the safety valve of retreat, it is likely that all parties will escalate to the point of harming each other (verbally if not physically), or to the point of painting themselves into a corner. A short retreat allows each person to regroup, focus on what the issues are, clarify what is and is not negotiable, and seek to resolve the issues at hand. Teach each other how to retreat prior to needing this strategy. Remember, this is not a technique for avoiding resolution. Rather it is a technique to allow everyone to calm down so that resolution is more likely to happen. Suggestions for successful retreats include identifying "off-limits" places for each person to retreat to and committing to a return after a reasonable period of retreat time.

Pressure Valves

Parents generally try to find a balance between setting challenging expectations for their children and providing support for their accomplishments. Sometimes it is difficult to find this balance. In these cases an outsider—perhaps even a professional—can be helpful in finding the balance. If the child feels that there is no way to be successful, this could indicate that the parents are having difficulty setting appropriate expectations. With excessive pressure the child may feel that there is no way to succeed.

Organizing

Many students who suffer from ODD also have difficulty with attention issues. Their lives may feel rather chaotic, and they may often appear to be forgetful or unconcerned. Simple organizational skills may help the ODD child feel more in control. A place for their things, a container for needed materials, posted notes and schedule reminders—all can play a part in helping the ODD student find ways to appropriately feel in control. Visible checklists, notes to all students near pass-by locations, and comments to the entire class about organizing may especially help those who have trouble with this skill, without singling them out.

Recognizing Compliance When It Is Already Happening

This technique is a rather sneaky way of training an oppositional child to feel that they are being compliant. Watch the child. Identify some behavior that is acceptable that the child is currently doing. Give the child a directive to do that behavior, then thank the child for doing it. Quickly move on to something else. Follow this pattern for a while, until you sense that the child shows some positive response to your praise. Then, pair a behavior that the child is not currently doing with the behavior the child is already doing. Praise the child for complying. There is a good chance that the child will continue to do the behavior they were doing on their own, as well as add the behavior that is new. This strategy is a form of compliance training and can be quite effective in avoiding open confrontation and opposition.

Relaxation/Anger Control Cards

Stress or anger management cards can be a useful tool to help students gain control of their own escalating emotions. These cards are similar to the mood rings of years past and work on the principle of body temperature. When we are in a "stress mode," our body responds with a fight or flight impulse. Part of this response is for blood to leave the hands and go to areas of the body that would be used in fighting or running away, i.e., the muscles. When the blood leaves the fingertips, the temperature drops. Students often respond to the "magic" of the directive to "change the color of the card." This process is a simple form of biofeedback and can be useful in helping students develop an awareness of their stress responses as well as the ability to begin to manage those responses. (Biofeedback cards can be purchased through YouthLight, Inc. at (800) 209-9774.)

Non-Verbal Skills that Increase Compliance/Reduce Non-Compliance

- Respect personal space – Stay about three feet away from the student
- Use a calm voice tone
- Use a low volume
- Eye contact should be brief
- Walk away, assuming compliance

The Early Bird

The earlier you intervene, the better. Two things happen as you delay intervening. First, everyone involved becomes less rational as a problem increases. For both the staff member and the student, anxiety kicks in, and everyone begins to be a bit more action-oriented and less thoughtful. Second, the potential for consequences increases, making intervention more demanding.

Because we anticipate a conflict, it is tempting to just "let this die down…" Unfortunately, often the issue escalates. Tuning in and re-directing the student early can prevent you from getting into the situation where you effectively have no control.

The Secret Desire

Everyone is more comfortable when the limits are known. Even though students often seem to resist limits, part of that resistance is a secret desire, through the discovery process, to determine exactly what the boundaries are. ODD students, just like everyone else, are looking for those boundaries. Clear boundaries reduce acting out. Fuzzy boundaries invite testing.

In the absence of boundaries and limits, students may act out to force the adult to declare the limits. An extension of that problem is that "good" students may support acting-out students when the rules are not clear. All students need to feel the safety of clear expectations.

Don't Just Stand There...Remove Someone!

When you sense the tension rising in a room, it sometimes helps to remove someone from the room. Surprisingly, it even helps to remove someone who is not actively contributing to the tension. The change in dynamics can slow down escalation.

Asking a student, including one not in trouble, to step into the hall for a minute creates a need on the part of other students to watch what is happening, and it also "normalizes" the experience of being asked into the hall. So, you may change the dynamics, thus avoiding a problem, while you simultaneously lay the groundwork for future problem-solving.

The Traveling Teacher

Walking into a student's area has an immediate impact on behavior. A smart teacher will become a classroom "traveler" by walking into all students' areas throughout the day. This approach is usually called "proximity influence." By simply walking into an area, you are able to impact the behavior of students. If the ODD student knows that you walk into EVERYONE'S AREA, then there is very little to complain about! This way, no student can complain about "un-special" treatment!

STRATEGY #104

Quick, Write Down Everything You Are Thinking Before You Forget It!

The ODD student may often come to you with a litany of intense complaints about someone. For students with writing or computer skills, an effective technique is to encourage them to write everything down before they forget the details. The writing process provides an outlet for this negative energy and helps a student feel "listened" to.

STRATEGY #105

Time Is On Your Side

Out of a sense of urgency we often make matters worse by invading the decision-making time that the ODD student often needs. If your impatient presence is non-verbally demanding compliance, the ODD student will read that and will resist it. Walk away; give it time. Often the student will feel the space to decide what to do and surprise you with compliance.

STRATEGY #106

Listen More, Talk Less

A surprise for those who want to be heard is that others often hear us more if we talk less. For the ODD student there is another twist to this—When we talk too much, we begin to sound as though we are trying to convince the listener of something. The ODD student picks up on this, stops listening, and starts resisting. So, practice good listening skills when the ODD student is talking. Let silent time happen. Then, briefly speak. You have increased the chance that you are being heard.

Distract then Redirect

This approach is particularly effective for younger ODD students. Move the attention to something else, perhaps to something curious on the other side of the room. Then, slip in your redirection comment. The time lag, and the focus elsewhere, can move the student into an "act first and resist later" mode.

STRATEGY #108

Staying on Your P's and Q's
(Persistent Questioning Technique)

Teachers would do well to use this technique when a student is misbehaving. Instead of using the typical response of too much emotion and too much talk, simply ask specific open-ended questions which will cause the student to answer questions about his or her behavior.

- What were you doing?
- What's wrong with what you were doing?
- What are the rules?
- What happens when you break the rules?

CAUTION: This type of questioning is not to be used as a "club." The goal is not to badger the student. Rather, the goal is to get the student to own the responsibility for his or her behavior without being overly confrontational.

Example: Let's make a plan to get what you want. List three things you are willing to do to accomplish your goal.

STRATEGY #109

Low-key Praise

Remember that ODD students really enjoy influencing your emotions. Whether your emotions are up or down, if the oppositional student is able to affect it, the experience is inherently rewarding. Therefore, when you give praise to ODD students, it often helps if you use a monotone, low affect approach. Be sort of matter-of-fact with your comments.

The Turtle Technique (for Grades K-3)

The goals of the Turtle Technique are to reduce impulsive and aggressive behaviors in young ODD students. When a child is getting frustrated or not acting appropriately, the word "turtle" is used to cue the young person to "crawl into his or her shell." The child stays in his or her "shell" until he or she is calm and under control.

In order for this technique to work, the child is previously taught to go to a designated place to relax and think about what to do. The counselor or teacher can rehearse this with the student several times and offer good suggestions such as having a specific "chill out" plan. If the child is taught a couple of relaxation methods (deep breathing, squeezing a stress ball, etc.), his or her time in the "turtle shell" will likely accomplish a lot.

Shield Technique

A key concept to impress upon youth with ODD is that they don't have to give their power away. In other words, they don't have to react in anger just because someone does something they don't like. Instead, a choice can be made to handle the situation in a sane way.

One smart option is to put up a "shield." The child or teen with ODD visualizes a shield in front of him or her. Negative comments such as name-calling just "bounce off" of him or her. Unjust criticism and anger provoking words move right on past. The "shield" represents a keen ability to not let others bother or disrupt a good day. He or she can choose how to best respond. In effect, he or she becomes great at the game of fencing.

Reading Your Messages

Every waking moment, each person is sending either "clear or muddy messages." Clear messages represent appropriate, positive behaviors. Conversely, muddy messages represent inappropriate, negative behaviors. Teaching the child or teen with ODD to monitor his or her "messages" toward others is a key step to improving relationships. Parents and teachers can serve as "coaches" to cue kids to recognize their messages and hopefully send more and more clear messages.

One other direction on this is to remind ODD kids to send themselves "clear messages." Kids with ODD have a propensity to be negative thinkers. Therefore, they ascribe "muddy messages" to themselves and situations that arise. Their goal should be to recognize negative thoughts (muddy messages) and change them to positive thoughts (clear messages). For example, the ODD kid might say, "I can't stand it. This stinks." Instead, he or she might say, "I don't like it, but I'll deal with it."

Anger Outlets

Objectives: 1. Students will learn three rules about anger.

2. Students will devise a plan to constructively release anger.

Materials: 1. Anger Outlets handout

2. Pencil or pen

3. Punching bag or pillow

4. Chill Out Bag—the Chill Out Bag may be ordered through YouthLight, Inc. at (800) 209-9774.

Motivation: Demonstrate positive ways to release anger with the "Chill Out Bag."

Lesson: 1. Discuss and memorize the three rules of anger that follow:

- You can't hurt yourself.
- You can't hurt others.
- You can't hurt property.

Discuss examples of each rule.

2. Remind students that it is O.K. to get angry. Everyone gets angry, but we can't lose control. With this in mind, inform students that today they will be making a personal plan to handle anger appropriately.

3. Distribute the accompanying handout called "Anger Outlets" to all students. Circle the "anger outlet" ideas that fit them. Note the open lines. Students may write their own ideas on these spaces provided they follow the rules of anger just memorized.

4. Now ask students to make their own "personal anger outlet plan" on their handouts. Ask students to narrow their plans down to three or four ideas they can learn to do automatically.

Application: Ask students to use the "Volcano Calendar" (Strategy #129) to monitor how well they are handling their anger.

Anger Outlets

Put a check by the activities that would help you get a grip on anger.

❑ Talk to someone you trust.

❑ Count to ten or higher.

❑ Hit a pillow or punching bag.

❑ Talk yourself through the situation *(self-talk)*.

❑ Take a personal time-out.

❑ Find a private place where you can go to calm down.

❑ Squeeze a stress ball.

❑ Read a good book.

❑ Listen to your favorite music.

❑ Exercise vigorously.

❑ Get alone and scream.

❑ Take a deep breath.

❑ Use a journal to write down thoughts and feelings.

❑ Take a one-minute vacation. Imagine going to a favorite spot or doing a favorite activity.

❑ Collect ice cream or craft sticks. Break sticks when you are mad or frustrated.

❑ Enjoy a pet.

❑ Draw or paint your feelings.

❑ Write a letter *(even if you don't send it)*.

❑ Clean or organize your room.

❑ Play a sport.

❑ Play with clay, Play Doh® or Model Magic®.

❑ Enjoy a hobby or special interest such as working on a collection or computer games.

Now make your own "anger outlets" plan. Narrow your list down to three or four strategies for handling anger.

1. _____

2. _____

3. _____

4. _____

Finally, commit your list to memory and use it when you feel stressed.

Anger Mapping

Objective: Students will learn to "listen" to their bodies in order to manage anger appropriately.

Materials: 1. "Anger Mapping" handout
2. Red markers or red pens

Motivation: Ask how many students participate in athletic activities. Ask what makes an athlete successful. After hearing the many responses, add another factor that probably wasn't mentioned. This is called "Listening to Your Body." Explain how athletes often have to pay close attention to how their bodies feel when determining when to push hard while exercising or easing up. For example, cramps are one of the body's symptoms that tell an athlete to back off. In a similar way, our bodies can tell us when our anger is getting too intense. Ask students what happens within the body when it is stressed by anger. List these ideas such as tight shoulders, heart pounding, sweaty hands, etc. on the body.

Lesson: 1. Distribute the "Anger Mapping" silhouette handout. Ask students to shade in areas on the body that signal to them that anger is mounting.

2. Have students share their results. Remind them that this is a form of "biofeedback," and it is their body's way of telling them to "chill out."

Application: Provide another "Anger Mapping" handout to each student. Ask the students to "listen" to their bodies during the next few days and record where they "wear their stress." Remind the students to ease up when these signals from the body occur.

Anger Mapping Exercise

Shade or color in the parts of the body where you feel stressed when angry or upset.

Name _____

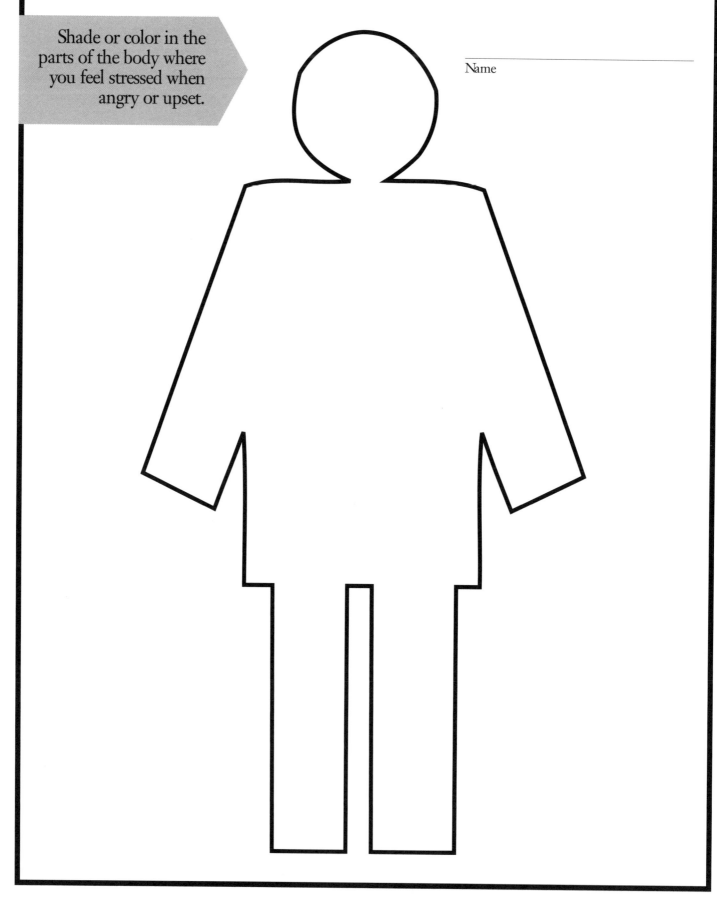

Chapter 4

Third Step: More Intense Interventions

This chapter covers more intense and persistent interventions. Many of the interventions covered in previous chapters should be part of the background for chapter 4 interventions. You may find yourself wanting to add these efforts when the intensity and duration of oppositional and defiant behaviors are higher.

Managing Anger

Oppositional and defiant students have the same life goals as most of us: to become independent, to learn the skills necessary to be successfully employed, to have the interpersonal skills necessary for satisfactory relationships, and, in short, to know themselves and make the most of their abilities. A significant area for everyone, and a particularly challenging one for students with ODD, is the area of emotional management. Understanding the meaning of and influences on emotions and learning the skills needed to deal with those emotions can make or break this challenging student in all life activities. In particular, managing the intense emotion of anger is a primary skill that students who are oppositional and defiant must master. This chapter begins with lessons on anger management.

Anger Incident Practice Sheet

Directions: Complete the practice sheet with as much accuracy as possible. Pretend you are recording this event as if you were a video camera with sound. A video camera couldn't show someone being mean to you. It could show someone calling you names.

1. When did you make yourself angry? *(What date and time was it?)*

   _____

2. Where were you when you made yourself angry?

   _____

3. Who else was present?

   _____

4. As specifically as possible, describe what happened.

   _____

   _____

   _____

5. What did you say to yourself to make yourself angry?
   (Hint - Listen to your thoughts and see if you can hear any demanding words
   like SHOULD, MUST, HAVE TO or OUGHT TO BE)

   _____

   _____

6. How could you change what you said to yourself to change your feelings?
   (Hint - Try changing your demanding SHOULD, etc. to preferences like I
   WISH..., IT WOULD BE NICE..., I'D LIKE.)

   _____

   _____

Helping Kids Deal with Anger Using Rational-Emotive Imagery (a.k.a. the "Make Believe Game")

What follows is an example of how rational-emotive imagery (REI) or the "make believe game" can be used with children and adolescents who have anger problems. This technique is most effective if there is a particular situation (i.e., the school bus, recess time, shopping trips) in which anger is likely to occur.

Start by having the child vividly describe the troublesome scenario. Get as many details as possible about the sights, sounds and events in this situation. Then have the child get as relaxed as possible in his or her chair with both feet on the floor.

PARENT: **"Amy, I want you to listen very closely to what I'm going to tell you. I want you to only be aware of my voice and focus on what I say. Try to block everything else out of your mind for the time being."**

"Imagine you are back in your class having problems with Mr. Smith. Picture the room in your mind. See all the posters on the walls and everything else that is in your class. Now go ahead and let yourself feel like you did that day. Feel all the anger you felt back then. Stay with that scene and try to feel just like you felt in the class. When you feel that way, wiggle your finger and let me know you're there."

(Author's note - It's a good idea to look for behavioral signs confirming that the child is actually feeling angry. The jaw may tighten, brows furrow and some children even make fists.)

"Stay with that feeling. Keep imagining that you are in your classroom."

(Author's note - Allow the child to stay in this state for approximately 20 to 40 seconds. Remind him or her to mentally stay in the situation and to remain upset.)

"Now I want you to keep thinking you are in the class but I want you to calm yourself down. Stay in the classroom in your mind, but try to calm down. Instead of being very upset, try to get calmer. Instead of being really mad, try to work toward only feeling irritated. Keep working at it until you can calm yourself down. When you can make yourself calm, wiggle your finger again."

Usually kids can reach a state of relative calm within a fairly short period of time. Once a child has wiggled his or her finger, it is time to bring him or her back to the here and now. Simply say something like, **"Okay, now open your eyes."** Next ask, **"What did you say to yourself to calm yourself down?"** If the child was able to calm himself down, he had to be thinking rationally. The only other way to calm down would be to mentally leave the situation (i.e., no longer visualize the classroom). This usually doesn't happen but if it does, try the exercise over encouraging the child to keep imagining the scene but working to calm down.

After completing REI, kids should then be able to tell you the thought that allowed them to calm down. A typical calming thought that might have been produced from the above scenario would be, "Even though I don't like the problems I've been having with my teacher, I can live with it. I don't have to like what he does."

Once the child has produced a calming thought, write it down. Now he or she can practice this mental imagery several times a day and use this same calming thought each time. In effect, this technique allows kids to mentally practice dealing with a difficult situation in a new, more productive way. It's very important that they practice this make-believe game on a regular basis if they are going to learn to handle their anger in a more productive fashion.

Usually children can learn to do REI by themselves after having been led through the technique a few times by the counselor or parent. It is also possible to make a tape recording of REI for the child to use at home. Some kids like using the tape rather than leading themselves through REI. Both can be effective if used regularly.

Individual Interventions

The following techniques are used helping ODD students cope with the anger that can be an ongoing problem in their lives. A majority of interventions are based on rational-emotive behavior therapy (REBT) which operates from the premise that emotions are largely the result of students' thoughts rather than produced by actual events. For example, students are not made angry by receiving a detention; they anger themselves with their demanding thoughts about the unfairness of the detention.

STRATEGY #117

Time Projection

When ODD students are angry, they often do not realize that with time, problems have a way of diminishing. Very few situations have lasting effects on students' lives. The purpose of time projection is to get the students to imagine the world after the event has become less important.

If an adolescent is extremely angry about a situation, encourage the student to imagine a month, two months or a year in the future. How much of an impact will this problem have on life in the future? Chances are the student won't even remember the situation; and, therefore, it is not worth the continual emotional upset he or she is currently experiencing. By getting the student to realize that this problem is a time-limited inconvenience, he or she is often able to keep a better perspective.

The Use of Humor

The use of humor and exaggeration can be used to show ODD students they are thinking in an irrational, illogical manner and creating their own anger. Humor can also be used to help establish rapport and "lighten" the mood when needed. Sometimes students get frustrated with the disputation process and even get angry at the person trying to help them.

Helper: "So you believe that Mrs. Smith has no right to give you a test right before Thanksgiving vacation?"

Mike: "She's not being fair. She always picking on me."

Helper: "Why not also demand that she let you look over the exams in advance? And why shouldn't you be able to take out any questions you don't like? How about letting you just write the entire exam? And grade it?"

By exaggerating the situation to a ridiculous extreme, it is hoped that the student will see it is unwise to demand anything that he or she doesn't have control over.

The Search for Control Technique

When students become angry, they are giving away their control over the situation. Nobody likes to feel as if they are powerless, and ODD students are certainly no exception. Many ODD students think that when they are getting angry, they are demonstrating power; but in actuality, they are exhibiting weakness. Here are a couple of ways of demonstrating this weakness.

When students state, "She made me so mad," try looking around on the floor as if you had lost something. When they ask what you're looking for say, "Your control."

Steve: "Are you looking for something?"

Helper: "Yes, your control."

S: "My control?"

H: "Somehow you've lost your control. We all have the ability to control how we feel, think and act but somehow you've lost yours. How else could someone make you angry?"

The same technique can be used with students who blame their difficulties on their "bad temper." It is not uncommon for students to blame their temper as an excuse so they do not have to accept responsibility for their behavior. Students say things like, "I've had a bad temper all my life," or "I've got a bad temper just like everyone in my family."

Melissa: "Are you looking for something?"

Helper: "Yes, my temper."

M: "Your temper?"

H: "I lost it about the time I stopped demanding that people treat me like I was king of the world."

Paradoxical Intention

Paradoxical intention can also be used with students who have anger problems. For example, if a student is extremely angry at another student, try to convince the student to try to act especially nice towards his or her agitator. Students often report they feel less angry. Also, behaving in this paradoxical manner could encourage the offending party to examine his or her behavior and act more appropriately in the future.

STRATEGY #121

Reinforcement

Reinforcement can be used in a number of different ways. For example, ODD children can receive rewards from their parents for attending school, completing homework assignments or for behaving appropriately in class. Some type of behavioral contract can be arranged regarding the reinforcement that can be earned for completing the agreed upon assignment. This type of program has the advantage of keeping the parents involved and aware of their child's progress.

Reinforcement can also be used as a means of encouraging ODD children to stay in control of their behavior. The above mentioned contract can include a section specifying the rewards a child can earn if he or she engages in appropriate classroom behavior. It is important to be behaviorally specific in terms of what constitutes "appropriate behavior." Parents and their child can work out an agreement that both sides can live with, but it is wise to allow the school counselor to have input on the contract.

Emotional Training

Emotional training can be effective when students are angry with other individuals. Ask students to recall pleasant experiences they have had with the individual(s) with whom they are now angry. Students are to imagine all the pleasant exchanges they had with this individual until the warm, happy feelings overpower the angry, hostile feelings.

This intervention can be given as homework and may be effective at keeping students from "stewing" and "ruminating" over negative feelings. In effect, this is reversing the process whereby intensely negative feelings are created. Rather than focusing on feelings of anger and hatred, they are focusing on pleasant memories.

Rational Role Reversal (RRR)

In RRR, the ODD student and helper switch roles. The counselor explains why others have no right to talk behind his or her back, and the student tries to get the adult to examine the rationality of his or her beliefs.

It is important to realize that an ODD child can have an intellectual understanding of concepts but may not have an emotional understanding or commitment. For lasting change to occur, the ODD child had better adopt these new philosophies wholeheartedly. RRR can be of assistance in this regard.

Helper: "Jimmy, I was wondering if you would mind if we did things a little differently today. I'm really mad about something, and I was wondering if you could try to help me work through some things."

Jimmy: "Okay. You mean I get to be the helper?"

Helper: "Yes. I'm mad at my wife. She told me before I left for work that I had to clean out the garage this weekend, and I had planned to go golfing with my friends. She has no right to tell me what to do."

Jimmy: "Why does she not have the right to tell you what to do? "

(Author's note—this response is a tactic the helper had used with Jimmy earlier.)

Helper: "Because I don't like it."

Jimmy: "Does she have to do what you like?"

Helper: "No, she doesn't have to, but she feels like what she wants is more important than what I want."

Jimmy: " How do you know that? Is it the truth for sure, or is that just what you think?"

(Author's note—this was also something the helper had said to Jimmy.)

RRR is helpful in two regards:

1) It lets the counselor know if the ODD student is understanding the logic of the counseling that has taken place. If the student is responding appropriately, it can safely be assumed he or she understands the concepts.

2) The responses the ODD students use with the helper clarify which interventions have been effective with the ODD child. Kids will use the words and thoughts that appeal to them. When the roles are returned to normal again, the techniques the student used should be relied upon by the counselor.

Rational Story Telling Technique

The rational story telling technique (RSTT) is a simple and straightforward intervention that can be effective with younger children. Psychiatrist Richard Gardner uses the Mutual Story Telling Technique, but his approach is from a psychodynamic perspective. RSTT incorporates the beneficial features of Gardner's work using REBT interventions.

As the name implies, RSTT involves having the ODD child and the helper tell each other stories. The rules are that the child always goes first, and the story can't come from a movie or television program.

The helper listens to the story and looks for the unhealthy, illogical ideas contained within the tale. The helper then tells his or her story making it similar to the child's but replacing the irrational ideas with rational thoughts.

The following story was told by a second grader who was having problems with peer relations at school:

Gary: "Once upon a time there was a big cow that lived in a farm field. None of the other cows liked to play with him, and he was really sad. The end."

Obviously, the cow in the story was Gary. The helper told Gary the following story.

"My story is about a big goat that lived in a forest. He also had problems making friends with other goats. Then one day he realized getting mad and butting the other goats wouldn't make the other goats like him. He also realized yelling and crying wouldn't make the other goats want to play with him."

"Instead he decided to nicely ask the other goats if he could play with them. If they said "no," he knew he didn't have to get mad. He could always ask some other animals. It took a while, but the other goats found out that the big goat was fun to play with. The goat was happy that he now had more friends to play with."

Not all stories are as perfectly lined up with the presenting problem of poor peer relations. The helper can always incorporate a positive message regardless of the content of the child's story.

Motivational Questions to Encourage Anger Management

This series of questions is designed to motivate the students to give up their anger or, at the very least, handle angry feelings in less destructive ways. Keep in mind that anger is a normal human emotion. There's nothing wrong with anger. It's what students do with anger that is important. Do students use it to make positive or negative changes in their lives?

What Has Anger Done for You Lately?

Simply ask the questions which are designed to help the student see the negative consequences of anger.

What has your anger ever done for you?

Has your anger made you any friends?	Yes	No
Has anyone ever paid you to get angry?	Yes	No
Has anger helped you have a positive reputation?	Yes	No
Has anyone ever told you, "I think you're really cool because you get mad all the time?"	Yes	No
Has anyone ever given you free pizza because you get angry easily?	Yes	No

What has your anger ever done for you other than get you into trouble?

SOS Team

S.O.S. stands for Seeking Other Solutions. This approach utilizes all the experience, knowledge, and skill of the school staff. Various members of the school staff clear their schedules one day a week to meet. This is a "sacred time" that takes precedence over all other meetings and activities for the time scheduled for this meeting. All support staff including the principal makes a commitment to be there barring an emergency. The input from the S.O.S. team is creative and practical. It allows the teacher(s) in the trenches to feel supported and not alone in the process of helping kids with behavioral and/or academic problems when making a referral. This is a safeguard for services being provided efficiently without duplication. Note the following outline of how an effective S.O.S. team works.

Goals
1. Brainstorming for ideas to help students who are having academic and/or behavioral problems.
2. Supporting the classroom teacher.
3. Referring students to appropriate resources.

Members
1. Principal
2. Counselor
3. School psychologist
4. Resource (special education) teacher
5. School nurse
6. Social worker (home-school worker)
7. Speech therapist
8. Behavior specialist
9. School resource officer

Process
1. Explore the background of the student and the problem(s)
2. Examine what has been tried
3. Discuss new options/interventions
4. Decide on a plan of action
5. Set a follow-up meeting date
6. Provide support and affirmation to the teacher(s)

Classroom Modifications to Encourage School Success

Many students with ODD are very frustrated in school. Learning problems obviously can create behavior problems, which may be avoided if students with special needs are set up for success. The following are classroom accommodations that do not lower standards, yet students can experience more school success and tolerate the educational experience better.

Seating
- Seat near teacher's desk
- Surround with good role models
- Avoid distracting stimuli
- Try not to isolate or make the child feel different
- Reduce stimuli area for quiet work time (for all students)
- Arrange desks in rows

Discipline
- Establish clear and observable classroom rules
- Review rules regularly
- Reinforce positive behavior
- Offer positive incentives
- Change incentives often
- Determine appropriate consequences consistently and in an unemotional manner
- Maintain consistency in daily routine
- Strong communication with parents
- Include students in setting rules and expectations when possible

Instruction
- Provide outline or key concepts prior to lesson
- Make lessons brief or break into segments
- Include a variety of activities
- Actively involve student during lesson (Summarize for class)
- Try to maintain eye contact during verbal instructions
- Stand near the student when giving directions
- Use behavioral cues to maintain attention
- Employ visual aids when possible

Directions

- Be consistent with daily instructions
- Avoid multiple commands
- Make directions brief and clearly stated
- Repeat directions in a calm, positive manner when needed
- Check for comprehension before the task is started
- Help student feel comfortable seeking assistance
- Use computer to assist written work if necessary
- Incorporate cooperative learning skills
- Utilize peer tutoring
- Monitor frequently; gradually reduce
- Use headphones to block auditory distractions

Assignments

- Abbreviate assignments
- Increase work time
- Highlight key directional words
- Rewrite directions at a more appropriate level
- Reduce number of problems per page
- Small group learning
- Provide manipulative objects
- Tape record materials
- Read orally if possible and necessary
- Use daily assignment sheet
- Write assignments on chalkboard

Testing

- Use dark black print
- Write clear, simple directions
- Underline key directions
- Provide practice tests
- Divide test into sections
- Test orally or tape record tests
- Give frequent, short quizzes
- Provide quiet environment for test

Connection, Competence, and Control

These are three ingredients to mix into the lives of students with ODD. Connection involves relationships. Adults who go out of their way to build a positive relationship with ODD children or adolescents often see improved behavior. Secondly, helping the student with ODD to find "islands of competence" is key. When a person finds something they like to do and are good at doing, this changes behavior. A purpose for waking up in the morning and a passion to do something meaningful can change a person.

Finally, giving youth with ODD a sense of control is a necessary ingredient. When ODD students are given an opportunity to be a part of the solution, they tend to be more cooperative. Ask, "What would make things better?" A sense of control goes a long way.

ACTIVITY #129

Volcano Calendar

The "Volcano Calendar" helps young people keep track of their progress. The number of times anger is displayed in inappropriate ways is tallied. A young person may have several displays of anger recorded in a day. The intensity or strength of the inappropriate display of anger is recorded on a scale of 1-10. Ratings of 1-3 represent low intensity, 4-6 represents moderate and 7-10 high intensity. This tool not only shows what progress is being made but also is a tool for accountability.

Volcano Calendar

Name _____ Month _____

Rate the <u>intensity</u> of each display of anger on a scale of 1 to 10.
Record each display of anger to note the <u>frequency</u> of occurrence.

Day	Anger Displayed	Intensity
Monday		
Tuesday		
Wednesday		
Thursday		
Friday		
Saturday		
Sunday		

The Weather Station

Think of your brain as being like a weather station with three possible weather forecasts. Just as the weather can have different conditions, the brain has different ways of thinking about life's situations. You can picture situations and things in life in a good or bad way. The choice is yours.

The first forecast in your brain calls for **cloudy weather**. The cloudy brain forecast looks at things in the worst way. You let things bother you and you don't feel good about yourself. You can't think clearly and let things or situations ruin your day. People who are in their cloudy minds get mad, worried, or upset and stay upset.

Now think about what you would do if you were worried about the weather forecast. Let's say that you felt unhappy about the current weather conditions. What would you do? Of course, you would look forward to better weather. In a similar way, when your brain is stuck in your cloudy mind, you can choose to create a climate for better weather. Imagine that you can cause better weather to happen by controlling the climate of your brain.

The next weather forecast is for a **sunny mind**. Sunny brain weather is when you think clearly. You don't let things bother you (at least not for long) and you feel good about yourself. You have a good ability to handle what comes your way even when things don't go right.

The third brain weather forecast is the **rainbow mind**. When you are on the rainbow forecast, your brain is full of good ideas. You can think of great ideas to solve problems in your life. You can solve not only hard math problems but personal problems as well.

Always remember that you can control your own brain's weather forecast. You can choose to stay in either the sunny or the rainbow forecast. If you find yourself in your cloudy mind, as we all do at times, remember you can change the brain weather anytime you wish. Make a special effort to create sunny and rainbow weather, and you'll be more relaxed and smarter than ever.

Here are some examples of the three brain weather forecasts.

Situation: You have a big test coming up soon.
1. Cloudy Mind – *"I know I'm going to mess up."*
2. Sunny Mind – *"I know the test will be hard, but I'll do all right."*
3. Rainbow Mind – *"I'll get with my friend who is real smart about this stuff. We'll study together, and then I know I'll be ready for the test."*

Situation: You're home alone, and you hear a strange noise.
1. Cloudy Mind – *"I just know someone is trying to break into our house."*
2. Sunny Mind – *"I heard a noise, but I always hear noises around here especially when the wind is blowing. It's probably nothing."*
3. Rainbow Mind – *"I'll check it out and see what the noise is. Then I'll know that everything is fine."*

Effective Directing

One of the most common complaints from teachers is that their students don't follow rules and/or directions. Teachers find that when they ask their students to do something, it often doesn't get done. Students may argue with them, refuse to comply and even become verbally and physically abusive.

At times, teachers have trouble getting their children to stop certain behaviors. For instance, they may find themselves telling students repeatedly to stop arguing or making unnecessary noise.

To effectively communicate, teachers must be firm, expressing consistent and reasonable expectations about the child's behavior. If the student would rather avoid whatever is being asked of him or her, then the teacher must not act as if they have a choice. If students feel like they have a choice, they will choose to avoid the activity.

While it may seem like they are being oppositional, if teachers are in some subtle or not-so-subtle way giving students a choice, they aren't really being disobedient.

Teachers accidentally give children choices when they say:
> *"Will you please stop talking?"*
> *"It isn't nice to hit."*
> *"When you grow up and look for a job, you will wish you did your homework."*

An adult who was being effective and assertive would say:
> *"I expect you to stop talking now. This material is important."*
> *"It is time to do your homework. Go to your desk and get started."*

Principles of Effective Directing
- Look your child in the eye.
- State your expectations in a direct and firm manner.
- If you don't want to give the student a choice, don't ask; tell him or her.
- Don't be sidetracked by excuses, whining, or arguing.
- Don't allow yourself to be manipulated by comments from the student.

Distraction

One of the goals when working with ODD students is to help them learn how NOT to become angry when things don't go their way. One of the simplest and best is distraction.

The ODD students have to think of something other than the situation they're getting ticked off about. This is more difficult than it sounds because when people are getting mad, the ONLY thing they seem to be able to think about is the person or situation that's bothering them. That's why ODD students need to decide what to think about BEFORE they start getting angry.

Encourage ODD students to pick "a scene" to think about before they get ticked off. This memory should be either the happiest or funniest thing they can remember. For example:

- The time they hit a home run to win a game.
- The best vacation they ever had.
- Their best birthday party ever.
- A time they had an unexpected day off from school because of bad weather.

Take a few minutes and think about the distraction scene. Make certain they've picked a good scene because it is important. Now they need to practice imagining this scene several times daily for the next few days. When they're sitting on the bus or waiting in line to eat lunch, have them just close their eyes and picture their scene as clearly as they can. Bring in all the details that they can possibly remember.

What were the people wearing?
What were the sounds around you?
Were there any smells in the air?
Try to make the scene in your mind just like watching a video.

The idea then is to switch to this scene when the ODD students find themselves getting angry. Instead of thinking their parents or teachers are acting like jerks, concentrate on the scene. Instead of getting mad because someone borrowed a dollar and forgot to pay them back, concentrate on the scene until the feelings start to subside. Whenever they feel themselves getting angry, switch to the scene.

THERE IS NO WAY AN ODD STUDENT CAN THINK OF A DISTRACTION SCENE AND STILL BECOME ANGRY. It is absolutely impossible. Since anger is produced by thinking demanding thoughts, thinking about a funny or happy memory will keep them from getting really upset. It will buy them time. That few seconds of time could be the difference between handling a situation and blowing it.

The Carol Burnett Technique

When dealing with an ODD student, keep in mind one of the distinguishing features is, of course, oppositional behavior. These are students who will resist attempts for compliance simply out of the desire to keep from feeling controlled. That is why normal behavior interventions often prove ineffective with ODD students. They will oppose just to oppose. And most of them are good at it.

The Carol Burnett Technique (CBT) is a behavior management technique that can be used to redirect a student's behavior without drawing attention to the student. If presented to the ODD student correctly, they often will think of CBT as a game rather than an attempt to control them. Therein lies the key to this technique . . . the presentation.

First, it is necessary to pick out a target behavior such as making excessive noise at your desk. It is necessary to select a target behavior that is clearly understood by both the adult and the student. Avoid vague targets like "following school rules." It's better to define the particular rule that is being violated (i.e., bother others by talking, calling out answers without raising your hand, etc.).

Once the target behavior has been established, have an individual conference with the student. Ask the student if he or she would like to play a secret game. Most students in elementary grades will love this idea. Emphasize that this game is going to be just between the teacher and the student. It's a secret and if both parties do their respective job, it can remain a secret. That's the goal, to see if you can make it work without anybody figuring out what you're doing.

The teacher should say something like, "You know how you've been having that problem with making too much noise at your desk? I've been having to tell you to quiet down because others are trying to work. I know you don't like it; and I don't like having to call your name all the time, so I have a plan. Instead of telling you to quiet down, I'm going to give you a secret signal. I'm going to touch my ear when you're making too much noise. That's the secret signal for you to quiet down. I'm not going to say a thing, just touch my ear from wherever I am. Okay? Let's see if we can keep this our secret."

It is possible to develop a contract for rewards if the behavior improves, but it's best just to let the plan, the secret, be the reinforcement. It's also possible to switch the target behavior if necessary. It would not be wise to have more than one target behavior for a student at any one time. Otherwise it could get confusing for the teacher and student.

The CBT works very well with elementary age students. By middle and high school, ODD students will view this intervention as just another way to control their behavior; and as a result, this would probably not be an effective intervention.

Body Cues Preceding Anger

There are certain things that happen in people's bodies right before they get mad. Many ODD students may not be aware when these "body cues" are happening, but it's important that they learn to recognize them. These cues are like a siren warning ODD students just before they go ballistic. By recognizing what happens to their bodies before they get angry, they'll have a second to distract themselves or walk away before they react.

Everybody has some kind of body cue that occurs just before they get angry. Here are a few of the more common ones. People say they:

- Feel warm all over
- Have sweaty palms
- Make fists with their hands
- Have stomach pain
- Have a clenched jaw and hold their teeth very tight
- Start shaking all over
- Feel their muscles get tight, especially in their arms

The knowledge of how a person's body feels just before he or she gets angry is important because it will allow a few seconds to think before reacting. Acting without thinking usually leads to bad results.

Triggers and Cues

*Name*_____

Outside Triggers:
What types of outside situations are you likely to get angry about?

1._____

2._____

3._____

4._____

Inside Triggers:
What types of thoughts are likely to make you angry?

1._____

2._____

3._____

4._____

Cues:
What happens in your body just before you get angry?

1._____

2._____

3._____

4._____

Rational Stress Management Form

1. Please describe the stressful situation. Be as specific as possible.

   _____

   _____

   _____

   _____

2. Your stress reaction

   Between 1–10, how strongly did you react? _____

   Your behavior (what did you do?)

   _____

   _____

   _____

3. Your stress-creating thoughts:

   _____

   _____

   _____

4. **Goals:**

   How would you like to feel?

   _____

   _____

   How would you like to behave?

   _____

   _____

5. New stress reducing thought:

   _____

   _____

   _____

Recognizing Depression

Grade Levels: High School (9–12)

Estimated Time: One or two class periods

Background: Depression is a serious health problem for thousands of adolescents. The more high school students know about depression, the better able they will be to understand and recognize it in themselves and their peers.

Materials:
1. Blackboard
2. Poster boards
3. *Internet

Procedures:
1. Begin the lesson by breaking students into groups of either 2 or 3 depending on the size of the class. The ideal number for groups is from 6 to 8 students. (3 minutes)

2. Ask the students what they know about depression. Do not be concerned about the accuracy of the beliefs at this point. List the beliefs on the board or poster board. (10 – 15 minutes)

3. Assign a particular belief to each group. They are to research the accuracy of the statement by finding articles in journals or magazines, books on this topic or go to the Internet. They are to determine whether the belief is a) True, b) False or c) Partly True, Partly False. (20 minutes)

Note that students accessing the Internet should have adult supervision.

4. Students are to prepare a poster detailing their findings. (20 – 30 minutes)

5. Students will then report their findings to the class. (20-25 minutes)

6. As a class, discuss what steps they should take if they themselves are depressed or if they suspect depression in a friend.

7. Display the posters in a popular location within the school.

Evaluation: Use the following Rubric to evaluate the posters and class participation of the students:
- **Three points:** Students were highly engaged in class discussions; they created comprehensive and thoughtful posters that included several relevant facts and quotes.
- **Two points:** Students participated in class discussions; they created somewhat comprehensive posters that included some facts and at least one quote.
- **One point:** Students participated minimally in class discussions; they created simplistic posters with few or no facts or quotes.

Treating Depression

Grade Levels: High School (9 – 12)

Estimated Time: One or two class periods

Background: Depression is a treatable disorder. This lesson is designed to help students understand the range of treatments available and their effectiveness.

Materials:
1. Blackboard or Dry Erase board
2. Poster board
3. *Internet

Procedures:
1. Begin the lesson by reviewing what students learned from the first lesson on depression. Once again, break the students into groups of either 2 or 3 depending on the size of the class. The ideal number for groups is between 6 and 8. Students can remain in the same groups, or new groups can be selected. (10-15 minutes)

2. Ask the students what they know about the treatment of depression. List the treatment options on the board or poster board. Make certain the list includes the following: a) peer listening, b) cognitive-behavioral therapy, c) the use of antidepressant medications, d) family therapy for the treatment of depression, and e) psychoanalytical treatment. (10 – 15 minutes)

3. Assign a particular treatment to each group. They are to research the type of treatment on the Internet* or in suggested resources. They are to a) describe the treatment, b) identify the theory behind this method, and c) describe the effectiveness of the treatment. (20-25 minutes)

   To access websites on this topic, use the following keywords: depression, mental health, bipolar
   Note that students accessing the Internet should have adult supervision.

4. Students are to either a) record their findings on a designated section of the black/Dry Erase/poster board, or b) prepare a poster detailing their findings. (20 – 30 minutes)

5. Students will then report their findings to the class. (20-25 minutes)

6. As a class, discuss the pros and cons of each treatment option.

7. Display the posters in a popular location within the school.

Evaluation: Use the following Rubric to evaluate the posters and class participation of the students:
- **Three points:** Students were highly engaged in class discussions; they created comprehensive and thoughtful posters that included several relevant facts and quotes.
- **Two points:** Students participated in class discussions; they created somewhat comprehensive posters that included some facts and at least one quote.
- **One point:** Students participated minimally in class discussions; they created simplistic posters with few or no facts or quotes.

Anger Management

Grade Levels: 2nd – 5th

Estimated Time: One class period

Background: Anger is an emotion that causes many problems in our society. Some people develop chronic health problems, while others become violent due to their inability to manage their anger. Students can learn to calm themselves using a variety of techniques.

Objectives: Students will be able to list three things that calm them down when they are angry.

Materials: Old magazines, glue, scissors, paper, magic markers, and crayons

Procedures: 1. Display things that help calm you down (such as a CD player, a book, and/or a basketball). (5 minutes)

2. Ask students to describe things that help calm them down. (5 – 10 minutes)

3. Ask students to describe times they made bad decisions when they were angry. (5 – 10 minutes)

4. Get into groups of 2 or 3 and describe things you do to calm down when you're angry. (5 minutes)

5. Explain that students will be given time to create a picture that describes the ways they calm themselves down when they are angry. Students can create a collage from magazines, draw pictures, or write a poem to describe the ways they calm down when angry. (20 minutes)

Evaluation: • **Three points:** Students were highly engaged in the activity; they created an expression of art that listed at least four ways they calm themselves down.

• **Two points:** Students participated in class discussions; they created an expression of art that listed at least three ways they calm themselves down.

• **One point:** Students participated minimally in class discussions; they created an expression of art that listed at least one or two ways they calm themselves down.

©Youthlight, Inc.

The Three R's for Rerouting Behavior

Objectives: 1. Students will identify behaviors that are problematic.
2. Students will learn to replace negative behaviors with more constructive behaviors.

Materials: 1. Worksheet
2. Paper
3. Pencil or pen

Motivation: Ask students to write a short paragraph about the worst trouble they have ever had at school. Write this on the accompanying worksheet in the "Reflect" section. Next ask for volunteers to share their stories and what consequences resulted from their mistakes.

Lesson: 1. Tell the students that today they will be learning the Three R's for rerouting or turning around behaviors.

2. Teach the following information.

Reflect – Go back over the situation thinking about what went wrong.

Rehearse – Brainstorm other responses in this situation that would likely have made for a positive result. Own up to any bad choices that were made.

Remember – A small item is chosen to carry as a constant reminder to handle new situations well. Items might include an anger control card, a smooth stone, a stress ball, a ring, etc. Be creative!

3. Ask students to fill out the "Rehearse" and "Remember" sections on the accompanying worksheet.

4. Have students discuss and role play their "Rehearse" responses.

5. Now have students share their thoughts about items they may use to remember their more positive behaviors and responses to situations.

Application: Ask each student to find the item of remembrance and carry it with him or her for the next week. After this week, allow students to discuss their results.

Three R's Worksheet

Reflect: I take responsibility for my behavior when I _____

_____

_____

_____

_____

Rehearse: I could have handled the situation better by _____

_____

_____

_____

_____

Remember: A small item I can carry with me to remember to handle things better is

_____

_____

_____

_____

No FAT Brain Food

Objectives: 1. Students will learn how to think constructively to overcome unpleasant feelings.
2. Students will learn to control emotional reactions.

Materials: Pictures or actual items of low fat foods.
Worksheet
Pencil or pen

Motivation: Discuss how eating low fat foods helps our bodies to be healthy. Hold up various low fat food items. Likewise it is equally important to take care of our emotional health. Therefore, today we are going to learn about "No FAT Brain Food."

Lesson: **1. Explain the following.**

While our feelings are a very special and important part of us, they can cause us big problems if we do not manage them well. Just imagine how many people would avoid you if you let anger control your life. Imagine if you let fear run your life, how it would trap you from going places and doing normal things.

Here's how feelings get us in trouble. It's called FAT.

Feel ➔ Act ➔ Think
(Write on chalkboard or overhead)

Let's say a person feels mad at his teacher. Without thinking through it, this person acts out by calling his teacher a "sad sack of manure." By this point, the feelings of anger and frustration are so strong that thinking clearly is hard to do. Our feelings have taken over, resulting in a likely suspension from school.

2. Further explain the following.

Now let's go to a "no fat thinking diet." In order to do this, we only need to rearrange two letters.

F A T ➔ F T A
(Write on chalkboard or overhead)

Now watch what happens. When the person feels angry about the teacher, his brain takes over. He thinks, "I know I'm right about this one, but I'll wait for the right time to make my point. In the meantime, I'll just have to 'bite my tongue'." With this clear thinking, the person goes on and copes with the situation.

Feel   (Noticing your feelings are normal)

Think   (Thinking clearly through the situation)

Act   (Acting wisely)

(Write on chalkboard or overhead)

Application: In the next several days, fill out a "No FAT Brain Food" worksheet the next time you feel anger or frustration. Remember to follow the plan.

Feel → Think → Act

Feel   **(List your feeling.)**

_____

Think   **(Write a smart thought about the situation that you used to work through the situation.)**

_____

_____

_____

Act   **(Write about what you did to handle the situation well.)**

_____

_____

_____

_____

_____

Chapter 5

Fourth Step: Comprehensive Supports

FROM SIX TO TWENTY-FOUR HOUR INTERVENTIONS

A pattern of severe oppositional and defiant behavior can escalate to the point where it is emotionally and/or physically dangerous for the student, the adult, and for family members. It may become necessary to provide the student with individually determined "wrap-around" supports and structure, to move the student to a special day school for six hours of structured support, or even to move the student into a setting that provides twenty-four hours of structure.

This last chapter describes some examples of the most intense and focused interventions.

Recognizing the Stages of Anger

While being in the midst of an outburst of angry expression may feel like a sudden event, upon examination it is clear that most such episodes start small, escalate, and eventually wind down. Often described as "the escalation cycle," or "the stages of anger," it is useful to train oneself to recognize the parts of this cycle so that one can maximize the effectiveness of responses and, at least, not make matters worse!

Different authors break the cycle into four to seven stages. For example, the Crisis Prevention Institute, Inc. (CPI—a comprehensive training program to help staff develop skills in prevention, de-escalation, and physical intervention) labels the crisis escalation cycle with four phases:

1. Anxiety
2. Defensiveness
3. Acting-out person
4. Tension reduction

Regardless of the number of "stages," the escalation pathway is similar in most descriptions. Following is a "map" to these stages. The numbered interventions are suggested behaviors and/or attitudes for the adults to take during the particular stage of the cycle.

Student Baseline Behaviors

This is the period of time that we might describe as "just normal." The child is behaving in ways that are acceptable and appropriate. In a classroom setting, the child might be described as "on-task." Because human nature is such that "the squeaky wheel gets the grease," we usually have to take special notice to understand the conditions under which a child behaves acceptably.

Adult role: Be aware of the circumstances surrounding appropriate behavior

Take note of the circumstances that support appropriate behavior with the student. Gauge the student's responsiveness to praise, feedback, and normal, social contact. If you are observant, you may be able to re-create the circumstances that surround this pattern of behavior.

Stage 1:   The Student Shows Irritability or Anxiety

At this time the child behaves in a way that is out of character. For example, a talkative child may be quiet, a normally outgoing child may have his or her head on the desk, or the child may be overtly "on edge."

Adult role: Show concern or support to the student

We may be tempted to "nip it in the bud" when a student starts showing these signs. Unfortunately, this tactic usually causes the student to get worse. The more effective response is to privately, quietly, and directly show concern for the student. You may do this through nonverbal means, through verbal means, or (carefully) through gentle touch. We have all had the experience where a friend comments, "…you look a little worried. Is there something I can do for you?" Even if there is nothing to be done, this simple show of concern makes us feel better and usually helps us refocus on matters at hand. And so it is with the student, even the ODD student.

Stage 2: The Student Reacts to Triggers and Shows Poor Awareness of Consequences

At this point the student probably does something sufficiently overt to get the attention of most others in the area. And often there is a wave of anxiety that washes over the area, because everyone takes note that this student has already stepped over the line. There is much more intensity as the student responds to the least provocation or, sometimes, to no obvious provocation.

The adult at this point realizes that the student is moving in the wrong direction. The adult may be realizing that the behavior displayed requires a discipline response, but to do so will probably result in more intense behavior.

Adult Role: Helpful Attitudes or Behaviors When the Student Shows Poor Awareness of Consequences

On some levels it is likely that the student also feels the potential of additional acting out and escalation. To help the student regain appropriate control, the adult should focus on directions that allow the student to make a decision, to make a choice, and to become engaged in some behavior that helps the student regain focus and organization. It is critical that the adult use the right balance of tone—too much, and the student skyrockets; too little, and the student turns on the adult. "Just right" will include the adult remaining in control of his or her own feelings and verbal/nonverbal communication. This is sometimes accomplished by giving the student two simple choices and an activity to become involved in. It may help to find a way to discreetly allow the student to leave the area so that peer observation does not muddy the waters. Because of the volatility of the student at this point, the adult should also consider preparing for the worst…

Stage 3: The Student Has a Loss of Control — a Meltdown — Emotional and Physical Release

Most people experience losing control at some point in their lives. The interesting thing about it is that, during the episode, you may have an out-of-body awareness where you are commenting to yourself, "I know this is terrible behavior, but they need to get a piece of me, they need to know how strongly I feel about this, they won't forget this, and they deserve it!" At the time, the acting out, whether it is verbal or physical, gets justified in one's own mind.

Adult role: Managing During the Meltdown

So what can you do at this point? Your only reasonable goal is safety. There is very little that you can do to get the student to stop. So you focus on safety and try to respond in ways that do not further escalate or prolong the event. Appropriate actions during this phase usually include isolating the student from others, making sure there is adequate assistance to maintain safety, and using safe, nonviolent means of restraint.

Stage 4: The Student Begins to Calm Down and Regain Rational Thought

Every storm eventually ends. But things are not quite the same as they were before the storm. There may be debris to pick up, things to repair, costs to be paid. So it is after the meltdown stage. At some point the student runs out of physical and/or emotional energy and begins to settle down. It is likely that the student will be extremely vulnerable at this time. He or she is beginning to remember the probable consequences of their behavior. The student is likely to feel embarrassed or feel the need to regain respect or to save face.

Adult Role During the Calming-Down Stage

The adult will want to remain calm, show concern for the student, and be steadfast regarding procedures. It will be helpful to make sure that the student is not injured and to meet other physical needs of the student. The student may want or need a drink of water and a chance to wash his or her face off. Clothing may need to be adjusted. Handling all of this with privacy and respect is paramount.

After the Crisis: Processing and Learning

When a student experiences a meltdown, the result is much like the Chinese symbol for crisis. Two symbols are combined: one for the concept of danger; the other for the concept of opportunity. And so, we have a student whose behavior has created the possibility of feeling worse, less than before, or feeling more emotionally and physically vulnerable. How do you increase the chances that the student can become more than he or she was before the event?

Adult Role: Respect, Review, and Respond

If there is clear intent to help the student feel in control by learning from the event, there is a chance, an opportunity, that the student may gain skills that will help in future events. Adult behaviors that help include calm discussion, a review or analysis of the event, the lack of berating the student, a focus on the student's best interests, and the commitment to follow through on predetermined consequences. ODD students notice when adults make promises they do not keep. Experiencing anticipated consequences contributes to the student knowing that the adult can be counted on. Also, some would argue that "paying for one's mistakes" removes an unspoken sense of indebtedness when others have been wronged. Some of these thoughts certainly are not conscious with the ODD student. But adults with experience and perspective often act on those bases, whether or not the student can articulate the reasons.

Physical Intervention

There are many times when we consider physical intervention when managing students. We may be tempted to use physical control to force compliance or to move a student to another area. But the truth is, *physical intervention should only be used for safety when other methods have failed.* The meltdown phase described above is an example of the circumstances that may require physical intervention.

The use of physical restraint will usually incite an escalation in resistant behavior. This is true for all students, but even more so for the ODD student. Because there is interplay between our anxiety and the behavior of the student, we can easily begin to think less rationally, temporarily convincing ourselves that, "…in this situation it is reasonable to use physical intervention."

If you are working in a setting or with a student where physical intervention is anticipated, you are strongly encouraged to obtain training from one of the quality nationally recognized de-escalation and physical intervention training programs. These programs include information on the cycles of escalation, appropriate ways to de-escalate an individual, safe physical techniques, and debriefing strategies following the event. The training programs are highly experiential in nature and generally require some demonstration of skill under quality supervision. Your safety, the safety of your students, and your legal position will be greatly enhanced from completing this training.

While there are a number of respected programs that are offered nationally and internationally, two of the more prominent ones are:

- Crisis Prevention Institute, Inc., 3315-K North 124th Street, Brookfield, Wisconsin 53005, 1-877-877-5389
- MANDT, 972-495-0755, MANDTSYSTEM.COM

Some of the principles that you will learn in training include:

Do practice the following:

- Use physical restraint for physical safety.
- Learn techniques in advance that are safe.
- Emphasize that you are helping the individual regain control.
- Rely on the team approach.
- Ask a co-worker to step in and help if you feel like you are losing control.
- Make sure that you are not in a situation where you are restraining the opposite sex without assistance or observation, particularly with older students.
- Be ready to release the student as they regain control.
- Be ready to help the student regain control.
- Recognize that the student will need to discuss the situation to regain a sense of respect and to be assured about your reasons for the restraint.
- Make sure to attend to any injuries.
- Document the event carefully and notify parents, guardians, and others.
- Talk out your feelings with someone who can give you support.

Do not do the following:

- Restrain if you are angry.
- Restrain to force compliance.
- Rely on students to assist in restraint of another student.
- Restrain if you risk significant injury.
- Restrain by yourself if a helper is nearby.

Service Learning Projects for ODD Students

The service learning component in education has increased in prominence in the past decade. Its popularity draws from the fact that service learning encourages students to:

- Apply learning principles to their environment
- Become actively involved in the learning process
- Explore and build upon their personal character
- Give back or provide some assistance to the community

In particular, service learning offers ODD students opportunities to develop feelings of capability and self-worth. Because of past concerns about ODD students, they are not often chosen for special roles and projects outside of the classroom. When provided with a clearly defined and supervised service opportunity, oppositional youth might surprise skeptics by excelling in their service-type work.

Sample School or Community Assistance Projects

- Create a care package for a needy student or family.
- Volunteer together to be "Meeters and Greeters" at PTO meetings.
- Adopt a pet. (Acquire parent permission and ensure who will be responsible for the future care of the animal.)
- Adopt a place on the school grounds to keep clean.
- Manage a booth at a school fair or carnival.
- Plant a tree, bush or flowers.
- Adopt a nursing home resident and visit him or her weekly.
- Make a presentation to younger students about a topic such as tobacco or alcohol/drugs. *(Make sure the lesson is age-appropriate.)*
- Assist a kindergarten teacher in the classroom.
- Construct something that a teacher can use in the classroom.
- Volunteer together for a fundraising activity.
- Assist with the school store, cafeteria staff, custodial staff, or office.
- Help decorate for holidays.

ODD Youth as Peer Helpers

Some oppositional youth have been successfully utilized in the roles of peer helpers or mentors. The key here is to ensure that sufficient training and supervision is provided for these young people. ODD youth have served with great success in the following roles:

Tutoring
- Read stories to young children.
- Listen to and help children read stories.
- Become a "Study Buddy" to another student.
- Encourage learning attitude by becoming a "Peer Pal" to a child.

Special Friend
- Write to a "Pen Pal."
- Become a "Big Brother/Sister" to another student.
- Assist a new student in school.
- Become a "Lunch Buddy" with a younger student.

Small Group Leader
- Lead a small group discussion with students in your classroom.
- Co-lead (with your school counselor) a small group for younger students.

Peer Mediation
- Participate in a mediation program where these students can help others in resolving conflicts.

128 ©Youthlight, Inc.

Networking

Gary Sibey II has long studied kids with disruptive behaviors. In his work he has identified two assumptions that kids with severe discipline problems typically hold. They are:

1. That others, especially adults, do not like them and are essentially undependable for meeting their needs.
2. That the world is unsafe, and aggression is the most effective means for protecting themselves from its hostility.

In an effort to break down this negative mindset, Dr. Sibey recommends a "multisystemic approach" for treatment. This approach has six facets that have specific goals in mind. They are as follows.

1. Play therapy

Aggressive, negative behaviors change with a safe environment and warm relationships. Play therapy offers a chance, maybe for the first time, for the youngster with ODD to experience a warm relationship with a therapist in a safe setting. During the process of play therapy, the person with ODD can begin to work through basic youth conflicts and learn to trust.

2. Parent training

Aside from helping parents with constructive forms of discipline, the main focus is on creating an "emotional connection" between parent and child. The goal is to center the parent-child relationship on something other than behavioral problems. Starting a new relationship is the hope. Remember, discipline without a relationship leads to rebellion.

3. School mentor

Kids with ODD need to make a connection with a school figure as well. This person becomes a "go to" person when things are not going well. This member does not "bail out" the ODD student when he or she is in trouble but is there to be a trusted adult who is a constant source of encouragement.

4. Community mentor

There is such a need for positive role models to steward their time to invest in kids. Mentors allow the person with ODD to see a "different world." Being around others who are going somewhere in life opens up new possibilities and hope.

5. Healthy peers

Poor behavior is reinforced by a deviant peer culture. To counteract this, three to four positive peers are selected to build a good relationship with a target youth. These three to four youths are trained to be peer facilitators. As the student with ODD builds relationships with positive peers, improved behavior is more likely to occur. The premise is that people tend to act like those around them.

6. Support system for parents

Parents of ODD kids need encouragement. Joining a support group helps them to see that they are not alone. Aside from receiving encouragement from fellow parents, many constructive parenting ideas are generated. Parents do not need to "reinvent the wheel." Instead much can be learned from each other.

Working with Children With Disabilities

There are some innovative programs around the country encouraging treatment for ODD/CD youth as opposed to simple incarceration. One program in particular has juvenile offenders working with handicapped children as part of their community service. In Los Angeles most of the adolescents involved are gang members with a long history of court appearances.

These programs need to be carefully monitored; but in some instances, the results have been remarkable. For many of these kids, working with handicapped children is one of the few times in their lives when they have felt loved and needed. In the words of one program coordinator, "Some of these kids put down a gun and picked up a spoon." Judges are always looking for creative ways of dealing with youthful offenders. They know locking up more and more adolescents is not the answer.

Pet Therapy

Father Flanagan's Boys' Home of Boys Town, Nebraska has many of their adolescents adopt a dog from the local pound to care for and train. These are animals that were scheduled to be destroyed. After the dogs have been trained, the animals are given away to families.

It may seem cruel to have the boys give away the animals after bonding with them. There is a good reason for this practice, and it has nothing to do with the logistics of taking care of the animals.

Think for a moment of the symbolism in this program. Here are boys, many of whom have certainly felt abandoned, caring for animals that have been rejected and cast out. With love and care, the animals go on to a better life with a new family. Let's hope the symbolism isn't lost on the kids.

Education Delivered in a Special School or Day Program

When the ODD student is persistently disruptive, either to his or her educational program or the education of other students, it may be necessary to temporarily assign the student to a special day school.

The potential benefits of such a placement include:

- A lower student to staff member ratio for more consistently available supervision and instruction
- More focused and consistent staff responses to behavioral issues
- The likelihood of staff skilled at aspects of behavior management
- The likelihood of staff skilled at social and behavioral skills instruction
- The ability of the program to "absorb" persistently challenging behaviors without employing questionable discipline techniques such as suspension, expulsion, and zero-tolerance
- The enhanced possibility of flexibility with the curriculum to increase motivation and success

Effective special school programs have certain characteristics, including:

- The school is not intended to be an experience in punishment
- A great deal of effort goes into nurturing student success
- The program is time-limited, with clear opportunities to return to the regular school setting
- Resources at the school communicate that the community/school district values the students and staff assigned to the school
- Parents are involved

An example of an effective special school follows.

Rebound Program

The Rebound program is a unique alternative for students who are not finding success in the regular school setting due to behavioral problems. This program offers a highly structured learning environment for at-risk youth ages eleven to fifteen. This particular alternative school is located in a rustic camp setting. The rugged outdoor setting fosters social, personal, and academic development as well as neutralizing behaviors that challenge authority. The Rebound program is designed to serve up to 200 at-risk male and female students in a full-time day program that operates throughout the school year. School hours are from 9 a.m. to 5 p.m. Monday through Friday.

Physical training, marching drills, and a rigid dress code are key parts of this program. Students dress out in a uniform and are led in exercises and marching drills by a trained military officer. This is a "marine approach" in that students are physically and emotionally broken down and then built up. Self-esteem grows tremendously through this demanding process. The drill officers are very demanding; however, the students come to learn that the staff cares very much for them. There are apt times for students to receive wise counsel and encouragement from staff members. This is truly a "tough love" situation.

An innovative and motivational behavior management is offered. Essentially, students have to work their way out of the Rebound program and back into the regular school setting. Beginning students start at the brown rank, signifying the ground level, and progress through various color levels. Ultimately, students progress upward to the blue and yellow levels. At the highest levels, these successful students mentor incoming students. Students are equipped in this progression to help other students new to the program.

Grade-appropriate instruction in language arts, math, science and history is offered. Computer skills and social skills training is an integral part of the school. Students with I.E.P.'s or 504 plans are kept on target with trained special education teachers.

The Rebound program has a success rate of higher than eighty-five percent—meaning students return to their respective schools and complete their course of studies. This has resulted from a unique partnership between the school district, the local police department, and the city parks and recreation program.

Model programs like this are available across the country, and more school districts are developing similar programs. Looking for options near you that are similar in nature are worth the effort for kids with ODD. For more information on the Rebound program, please call the following number: 803-981-1087.

Parenting Classes

One of the most effective strategies when working with inconsistent parents is to offer parenting classes. This is a tremendous amount of work; but if educators can teach parents to be better at managing their children, then schools can prevent future problems. The research is overwhelming in support of the belief that preventing problems is a lot more effective than trying to fix troubles after they occur.

One Wisconsin school district offered parenting classes in the fall and spring. The programs were based around the work of Foster Cline and Jim Fay, authors of the Parenting with Love and Logic curriculum. After a few sessions of classes, the curriculum became a collection of the best lessons from a number of programs.

The fall program was in the evening from dinnertime until around 8 p.m. The spring sessions were during the school day to accommodate second shift families. While parenting classes were a lot of work, it was very gratifying to see some of those efforts pay off. The sessions allowed plenty of time to discuss issues, get feedback from other parents, and also come up with workable solutions. Parenting is such a difficult set of skills that it's not something most of the individuals in classes could learn from reading a book. In all honesty, most of the parents wouldn't read a book anyway, so having a coordinated set of lessons was a must if there was any hope of changing parenting practices.

Research has demonstrated the efficacy of a particular model of family treatment known as Parent Management Training (PMT), which is a system that teaches parents to manage their child's behavioral problems in the home and at school. In PMT, parent-child interactions are modified in ways that are designed to promote pro-social, compliant behavior and to decrease antisocial or oppositional behavior. Initially, parents are trained to have periods of positive play interaction with their child. They then receive further training to identify the child's positive behaviors and to reinforce these behaviors. In effect, parents are trained to "catch the child being good." At that point, parents are trained in the use of brief negative consequences for misbehavior. Treatment sessions provide the parents with opportunities to practice and refine the techniques. Randomized controlled trials have found that PMT is more effective in changing antisocial behavior and promoting pro-social behavior than many other commonly used treatments (e.g., relationship, play therapy, family therapies, varied community services) and control conditions such as waiting-list or "attention-placebo" (Feldman & Kadzin, 1995).

Closing Comments

Getting to the end of this book does not represent having a final and conclusive "grip" on how to work with students with oppositional and defiant behaviors. It may represent having taken the time to let go of some dysfunctional ways of responding to these students. It may also mean that you have enough "staying power" to try understanding the range of techniques, and the dynamics of student behavior that they represent.

In the beginning of this book there was a discussion that concerned how the ODD student thinks and responds to the social world around him or her. Those thoughts are significant enough to repeat them here:

- I am the equal of those in authority—no one has the right to tell me what to do.

- Yes, I sometimes do the wrong thing, but it is usually your fault.

- When you punish or reward me, I feel that you are trying to control or manipulate me.

- Because I know how much you want me to change, I will be very stubborn about changing behaviors. In spite of experiencing your intended punishments and/or rewards, if I change, it will be on my time and for me!

- My greatest sense of control comes from how I make others feel.

Another statement from the same earlier section of the book also warrants repeating:

Interestingly, the eight characteristics that comprise a diagnosis of ODD are all behaviors or attitudes that only exist in relation to others, principally in relation to authority figures. This reality underscores the importance of the authority figure's own behaviors and attitudes in determining how instructive or destructive the situation with the ODD student will become.

It becomes clear that the opportunity to work with and to help these students depends on the abilities of adults to modify their own behaviors. And the good news is that if we do that, students with oppositional and defiant behaviors can get better. In fact, some studies show that as many as 25% of students identified as ODD will no longer qualify for the label within five years. It is the hope of the authors that this book will help raise those numbers.

References

American Psychiatric Association. (1980). *Diagnostic and statistical manual of mental disorders* (3rd ed.). Washington, DC: Author.

American Psychiatric Association. (1987). *Diagnostic and statistical manual of mental disorders* (3rd ed., rev.). Washington, DC: Author.

American Psychiatric Association. (1994). *Diagnostic and statistical manual of mental disorders* (4th ed.). Washington, DC: Author.

Angold, A., & Costello, E. J. (1996). Toward establishing an empirical basis for the diagnosis of oppositional defiant disorder. *Journal of the American Academy of Child and Adolescent Psychiatry*, 35, 1205-1212.

Angold, A. and Costello, E. (1993). Depressive comorbidity in children and adolescents: Empirical, theoretical and methodological issues. *American Journal of Psychiatry*, 150(12), 1779-91.

Atkins, M. S., McKay, M. M., Talbott, E., & Arvanitis, P. (1996). DSM IV diagnosis of conduct disorder and oppositional defiant disorder: Implications and guidelines for school mental health teams. *School Psychology Review*, 25, 274-283.

Beck, A. and Shaw, B. (1977). Cognitive approaches to depression. In A. Ellis and R. Grieger (Eds.) *Handbook of rational-emotive therapy*. New York: Springer Press.

Bernard, B. (1993). Fostering resiliency in kids. *Educational Leadership*, 51(3), 44–48.

Bernard, B. (1995). Fostering resiliency in urban schools. In B. Williams (Ed.), *Closing the achievement gap: A vision to guide change in beliefs and practice* (pp. 65-80). Oak Brook, IL: Urban Education National Network, North Central Regional Educational Laboratory.

Bowman, R.P. & Bowman, S. (1997). Co-Piloting: A systematic mentoring program for reaching and encouraging young people. Chapin, SC: YouthLight, Inc.

Brier, N. (1994). Targeted treatment for adjudicated youth with learning disabilities: Effects on recidivism. *Journal of Learning Disabilities*, 27(4), 215–222.

Brooks, R. (1992, Fall, Winter). Fostering self–esteem in children with ADD: The search for islands of competence. *Chadder*, pp. 14–15.

Brooks, R. (1994). Children at risk: Fostering resilience and hope. *American Journal of Orthopsychiatry*, 64(4), 545–553.

Brooks, R. (1994). Enhancing self–esteem in children and adolescents with ADHD. *The ADHD Report*, 2(3), 8–9.

Bushweller, K. (1995). The resilient child. *The American School Board Journal*, 182(5), 18–23.

Chaskin, R., & Rauner, D. (1995). Youth and caring. *Phi Delta Kappan*, 76(9), 667–674.

Dishion, T. J., Patterson, G. R., Stoolmiller, M., & Skinner, M. L. (1991). Family, school, and behavior antecedents to early adolescent involvement with antisocial peers. *Developmental Psychology*, 27(1), 172–180.

Farrington, D. (1987). Schools and delinquency prevention. *Today's Delinquent*, (pp. 71–86). Pittsburgh, PA: National Center for Juvenile Justice.

Feldman, J. & Kazdin, A. E. (1995). Parent management training for oppositional and conduct problem children. *The Clinical Psychologist*, 48(4), 3-5.

Frick, P. J., Lahey, B. B., Christ, M. A., Loeber, R., & Green, S. (1991). History of childhood behavior problems in biological relatives of boys with attention-deficit hyperactivity disorder and conduct disorder. *Journal of Clinical Child Psychology*, 20(4), 445–451.

Gibbs, W. (1995). Trends in behavioral science: Seeking the criminal element. *Scientific American*, 272(3), 100–107.

Gottfredson, D. (1984). *Environmental change strategies to prevent school disruption*. Washington, DC: Department of Justice.

Gottfredson, D. (1986). *Promising strategies for improving student behavior*. Paper prepared for the Conference on Student Discipline Strategies of the Office of Educational Research and Improvement. Washington, DC: U. S. Department of Education.

Greene, R., Biederman, J., Zerwas, S., Monteaux, M., Goring, J., & Farone, S. (2002). Psychiatric comorbidity, family dysfunction, and social impairment in referred youth with oppositional defiant disorder. *American Journal of Psychiatry*, 159(7), 1214-1224.

References *(continued)*

Hawkins, J. (1995). Controlling crime before it happens: Risk–focused prevention. *National Institute of Justice Journal*, 229, 10–18.

Katz, M. (1994 May). From challenged childhood to achieving adulthood: Studies in resilience. *Chadder*, pp. 8–11.

Katz, M. (1995, November). *From challenged childhood to successful adulthood: Studies in resilience.* Paper presented at the CH.A.D.D. Seventh Annual Conference for Parents, Educators, and Health–Care Professionals, Washington, DC.

Keilitz, I., & Dunivant, N. (1986). The relationship between learning disability and juvenile delinquency: Current state of knowledge. *Remedial and Special Education*, 7(3), 18–26.

Kohn, A. (1993) *Punished by rewards*. Boston: Houghton Mifflin Company.

Kuhne M., Schacher, R., & Tannock, R. (1997) Impact of comorbid oppositional or conduct problems on attention-deficit hyperactivity disorder. *Journal of the American Academy of Child and Adolescent Psychiatry*, 36(12), 1715-1725.

Martinez, A., & Bournival, B. (1996). ADHD: The tip of the iceberg? *The ADHD Report*, 3(6), 5–6.

Shaw, G. (1992). Hyperactivity and creativity: The teacit dimension. *Bulletins of Psychonomics Society*, 30 (2), 157-160.

Stoneman, A., Brody, G. H., & Burke, M. (1989). Marital quality, depression, and inconsistent parenting: Relationship with observed mother-child conflict. *American Orthopsychiatric Association*, 59(1), 105–117.

Sylwester, R. (1995). *A celebration of neurons: An educator's guide to the human brain*. Alexandria, VA: Association for Supervision and Curriculum Development.

Thornberry, T. (1994). Risk factors for youth violence. In L. McCart (Ed.), *Kids and Violence* (pp. 8–14). Washington, DC: National Governors Association.

Viadero, D. (1995 May/June). Research: Against all odds. *Teacher Magazine*, pp. 20-22.

Webster-Stratton, C. (1989). The relationship of marital support, conflict, and divorce to parent perceptions, behavior, and childhood conduct problems. *Journal of Marriage and the Family*, 51, 417–430.

Wexler, as cited in Wexler, H. (1996). AD/HD substance abuse and crime. *Attention*, 2(3), 27–32.

Wright, L. (1995, August 7). A reporter at large: Double mystery. *The New Yorker*, pp. 45–62.